Unforgettable walks to take before you die

Unforgettable walks to take before you die

Steve Watkins and Clare Jones

FIREFLY BOOKS

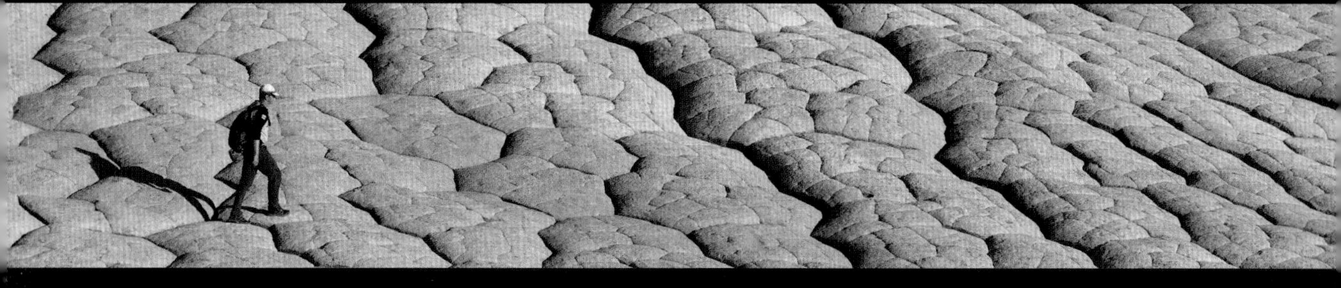

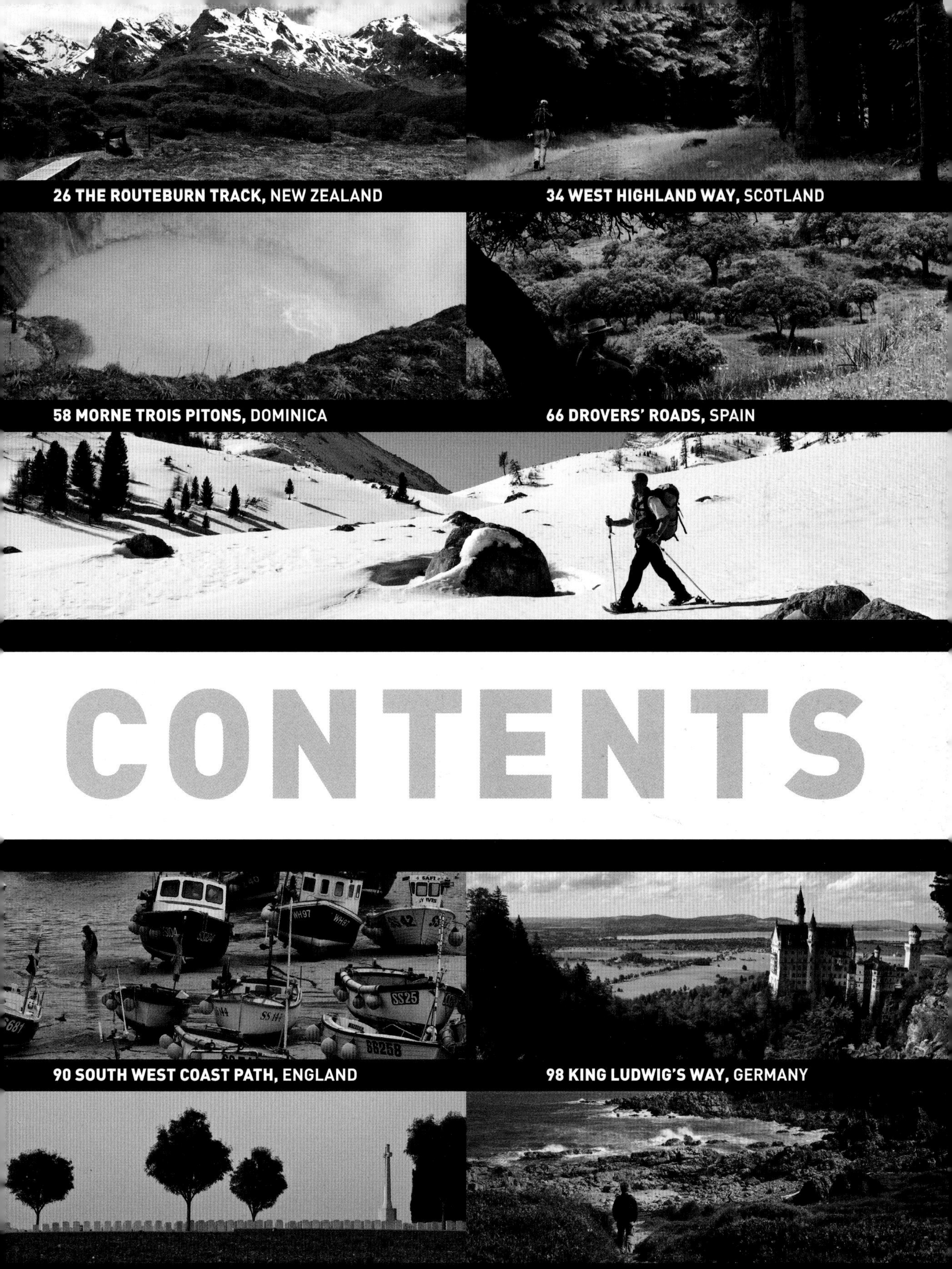

CONTENTS

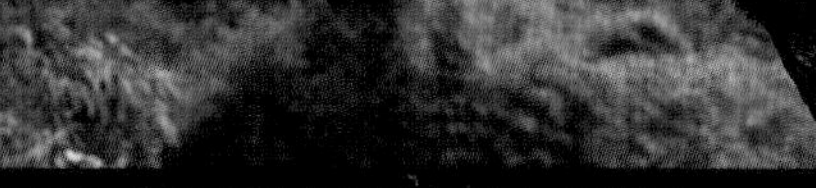

Introduction

The hectic pace of modern-day life often leaves us hankering after the chance to escape; to slow down, take a deep breath and soak up the simple and immediate details of our surroundings. If there is an art to travelling, walking can justifiably lay claim to being the most refined, as well as the most ancient, mode of getting around. This ultimate form of slow travel allows us to dictate how far we go, how long we linger and how much we see. By choosing to walk, which naturally engages both body and mind, we sense everything around us more acutely, and can have a deeper, healthier and more revitalizing travel experience.

Another appeal of donning walking shoes or boots is that there are endless opportunities and options to suit just about us all, no matter what our level of fitness. Walks can range in diversity from a gentle stroll through American history along Boston's Freedom Trail or a spiritual journey among the temples and shrines of Kyoto, to more committing adventures, such as traversing the Mont Blanc massif in the European Alps or climbing Mount Kilimanjaro. Even the more challenging trails are increasingly attracting relatively novice walkers, a sure sign that there is today a widespread and deep-seated desire to engage with the wild places on the planet. When the German climber Hans Meyer became the first person to stand on the summit of Mount Kilimanjaro in 1889, he could not have envisaged the tens of thousands of people who now do the same every year.

With so many choices, it was difficult for us to decide which 30 walks to include. All the ones we selected are accessible to anyone with the relevant fitness levels – you don't need to be a technical mountaineer for any of them – and they can be completed within at most two weeks; the majority require one week or less. Although you can opt to carry your own equipment, all the walks are available as organized tours, some guided, some self-guided. The Useful Web Addresses section on pages 254–5 lists their operators. These are the ones we used while researching the book and their services will invariably add a welcome touch of comfort and convenience to your walk.

We wanted to include not only some of the world's best-known walks, such as the Inca Trail in Peru and the Coast to Coast walk in England, but also some more unusual destinations, like the Karst country of Slovenia, which takes you back into a bygone age, and the trails around Fallingwater, Frank Lloyd Wright's outstanding example of how architecture can combine with nature, in Pennsylvania, USA. Our selection is not in any way meant to be definitive, nor is it laid out in any sort of ranking priority. Of course, we have our personal favourites, but everyone will experience the walks in different ways, so lace up your boots and get out exploring some of them if you can – the map on pages 252–3 will help you to locate them. This book is not designed to be a guidebook to trails and paths; rather, our intention is to give you a taste of what it is like to walk them. There are many excellent route guides and maps that give detailed descriptions of where to turn right and left.

Although walking is an ideal pace for taking photographs, our schedule did not allow us to hang around for days or weeks waiting for perfect weather. We undertook the walks just as anyone else would, and experienced the full range of what Mother Nature has to offer: the light of the midnight sun under clear skies in the Lofoten Islands; pelting rain on the Inca paving stones along the Takesi Trail in Bolivia; gale-force winds on the cliffs of England's South West Coast Path and glorious sunshine on the Routeburn Track in New Zealand. We may have flinched when things got wild but, thankfully, our camera equipment and sense of humour survived.

Some of the weather patterns we experienced served as reminders that extraordinary changes to our planet are occurring and that our fragile environment needs protecting. Given the heightened fears for the health of the Earth, it is, for some, becoming harder to reconcile these with flying to long-distance destinations. Awareness of global warming and the impact of air travel makes it difficult to feel that catching a plane is environmentally viable. But understandably, given the many wonderful and inspiring places the world has to offer, people still want to see them, to explore and experience them.

First-hand knowledge of the beauty of the planet can be the motivating factor for changing our way of life. At home, altering our shopping habits or means of transport, recycling, and being careful about the way we use water can seem inconvenient. Travelling often puts us in step with a very different world. We naturally eat only what is grown locally in Bolivia, happily explore Amsterdam on foot and conserve water in drought-stricken Australia. Perhaps these are some of the more valuable lessons we learn and bring back to our own lives, helping us to take small steps to change and improve the world around us.

Should you choose a long-haul destination, once you reach it the impact you make by walking is far less than that of any other form of travel. Depending on where you live, in this book there are, hopefully, walks that can be accessed without the need to board a plane. The choice of walking as a way of travelling is perhaps as good an interim answer to environmental problems as there can be – our way to leave only a light footprint.

Steve Watkins and Clare Jones, 2008

Yellowstone National Park
USA

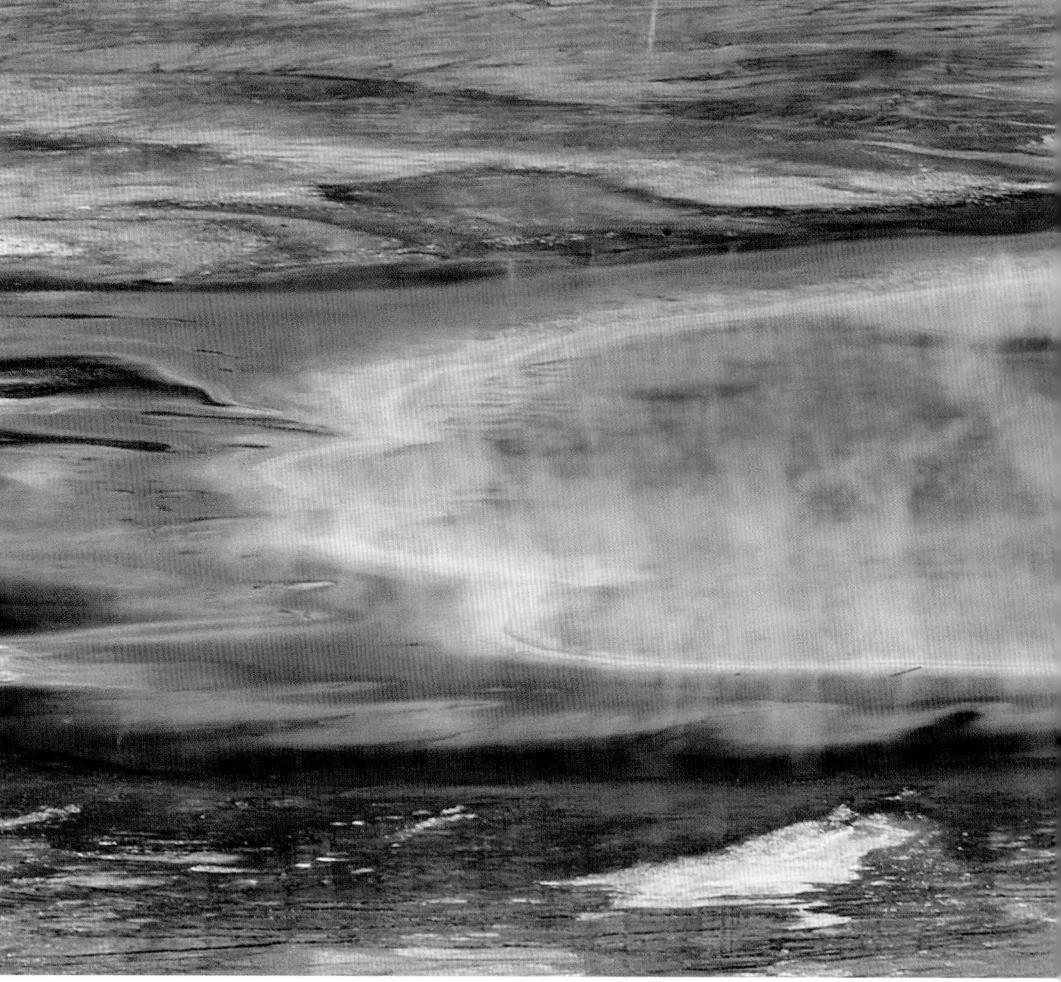

Steam swirls above Grand Prismatic Spring

In the centre of one of the world's largest-known volcanic calderas, Yellowstone National Park is a bubbling, hissing, surreal landscape teeming with iconic North American wildlife. From sweeping plains, high mountains and deep canyons to boiling rivers, explosive geysers and thundering waterfalls, its geographical variety is perhaps without equal – and its extensive network of trails, for both day walks and longer backcountry trips, make it a hiking wonderland.

Established in 1872, following several exploratory expeditions and lobbying of Congress, Yellowstone was the world's first national park and is more popular now than at any stage in its history, with around three million visitors a year. Thankfully, most of these don't venture far, if at all, from their cars, which makes walking the perfect way to explore, and get a feel for, the truly wild Yellowstone.

Throughout geological history there have been three major eruptions in the Yellowstone region; the most recent was 600,000 years ago and created the 72 km by 48 km caldera. These cataclysmic events were powered by the same heat and energy that today fuel over 300 geysers inside the park – two-thirds of all those on the planet – as well as numerous hot springs, mud pots and other geothermal features.

A gentle introduction, especially if you enter Yellowstone from the north entrance at Gardiner, is to take a walk around the Mammoth Hot Springs area. One of the park's multi-tiered boardwalks – common features on its more accessible trails, these reduce environmental impact and allow access to otherwise dangerous geothermal areas – winds its way up through an extravagant cascade of brilliant white, travertine terraces and steaming, thermal springs.

On the trail to Fairy Falls

Rainbow at Upper Falls on Yellowstone river

Bison are a common sight around Yellowstone

One of the most dramatic features in the park is the Grand Canyon of Yellowstone – a vertiginous, 366-metre-deep, 32-km-long fissure, carved largely by the Yellowstone river and otherwise by glacial action. The South Rim Trail makes for an exciting and relatively easy half-day hike and gives sensational views of the canyon's two pounding waterfalls: Upper Falls and Lower Falls. The path at first weaves its way through open forest. As it nears the Upper Falls there are viewpoints where, on a sunny afternoon, rainbows can be seen dancing across the plumes of spray thrown out from the cascade.

If you are reasonably fit, a side trip, Uncle Tom's Trail, will take you down an almost vertical set of 328 steps into the base of the canyon for incomparable close-up views of the Upper Falls. The testing return ascent is definitely one to take slowly. From the top of the steps, the main trail continues to Artist Point. This is the most famous place to view the canyon and the Lower Falls, a thunderous torrent that plunges 94 metres through a V-shaped cleft into the canyon. It is a lost world, where lone trees cling for life to the cliff face and the steaming azure and emerald river glows in the late afternoon with reflected light from the golden walls.

If you venture further south in the park, there will probably be encounters with bison and elk, especially around Firehole river and Geyser Basin where flatlands prevail. In the Midway Geyser Basin, another excellent and relatively easy half-day trail passes the outrageously coloured Grand Prismatic Spring en route to Fairy Falls, an enchanting, wispy cascade near the head of Fairy Creek. Soon after the start of the walk the spring comes into sight – a dense curtain of pink and blue steam rising on the horizon. Surrounded by blindingly white flats dotted with skeletal trees, Grand Prismatic is the third-largest hot spring in the world. It is an experience to see it from the ground, but to see it at its most spectacular it is necessary to work a little. Along the trail there is a series of small hillocks with indistinct, steep paths that take you up for a staggering aerial view of

Boiling pool in Firehole river basin

Desolate landscape at Mammoth Hot Springs

Boardwalks allow access on to fragile areas at Mammoth Hot Springs

the blue waters and the brilliant green, yellow, orange and rust-red fringes of the spring – colours created by bacteria growth.

Beyond the spring, the trail to Fairy Falls narrows and passes through young lodgepole pines overshadowed by legions of towering charred, black trunks. This area was badly damaged in 1988 during extensive wild fires that destroyed over one-third of the park. Tucked away in a scalloped alcove of grey rock, Fairy Falls tumbles serenely from the lip of the Madison Plateau. In free fall for much of its 60-metre descent, it eventually splashes gracefully on to darker rocks below, spreading across them into countless ephemeral rivulets.

Previous pages: Grand Prismatic Spring Dusk over Geyser Basin

A more remote geyser experience than the park's perennial favourite, Old Faithful, can be found along the road to West Thumb. The trail to Lone Star Geyser, an 8-km return hike, passes through lush, old-growth forest, untouched by the 1988 fires, and alongside the upper reaches of the tranquil Firehole river. It is a beautiful and easy walk, starting at Kepler Cascades, and if you time it right you may see the geyser in action. Every few hours it erupts into a 14-metre-high jet of boiling water. And here, unlike at Old Faithful, the chances are you will be alone, seeing the wild heart of Yellowstone.

ⓘ

In Yellowstone it is necessary to be alert for the presence of bears and other wildlife, such as bison and elk. Full guidelines are available at the ranger stations. Much of the park is accessible only from June to September, as snow covers the ground and roads for the rest of the year. Backcountry trails require permits to access and take several days to hike; they are very committing and require experience. If you only have a few days in the park, the day-hike trails, which don't require permits, are the best way to sample Yellowstone's various features. Accommodation inside the park is very limited and usually booked up many months in advance. There are more options in the towns around the four park entrances.

Evening light at Grand Prismatic Spring

Mediterranean Sea from path to Ravello

Amalfi Coast
Italy

Positano clings to the cliffs

Clinging precariously to the steep cliffs and terraces of the Lattari Mountains, villages along the Amalfi coast seem to need only a gentle nudge to send them tumbling into the Mediterranean Sea below. Soaked in Roman, Greek and Byzantine history, and with an inexhaustible supply of gourmet food and wine, the coastline is a relatively little-known walking delight.

Stretching for around 70 km from Sorrento, south of Naples, to Salerno, the coast is renowned for its dramatic road, which twists its way above precipitous drops. The severe terrain you pass through hardly suggests walking as a pleasurable way to explore, but a network of ancient, stone stairways and paths threads its way along the coastline, through the villages and above the cliffs into the beautiful green hinterland.

Amalfi, the pretty little port that gives its name to this part of the coast, is an ideal hub from which to access some of the area's best walks. Strung out along the mouth of a deep gorge and up its sides, the town is riddled with contorted passages and stairways, which in themselves make for intriguing exploration. The main street is dominated by the glittering, gold and columned façade of Sant'

Andrea Cathedral, from where narrow steps lead below the broad cathedral steps on to a balcony walkway to Atrani, the neighbouring village. Far quieter than its popular neighbour, it is set along a narrow beachfront and punctuated at its eastern end by the Santa Maria Magdalena Church set high upon a rocky outcrop jutting into the sea.

From the church, an impressive stone staircase leads ever upwards towards the village of Ravello, which makes for a good half-day round-trip walk from Amalfi. Perched atop a long promontory,

Lemons on sale in Amalfi market

Mules are used to transport goods to villages

Ravello is widely considered to be the most cultured pearl of the Amalfi coast. Its spacious, cobbled main square is a hive of activity by late morning and the swanky cafés around its fringes are the places to be seen. There are several options for walking back to Amalfi, or buses and taxis await anyone with weary legs.

For those with bundles of energy, an excellent extension to the walk – making it a full day – takes you into the beautiful nature reserve at Valle delle Ferriere, inland from Ravello. The path contours below spectacular cliffs, through enchanting woodland and past streams and small waterfalls before it emerges in the village of Pogerola.

Amalfi port

Santa Maria Magdalena Church, Atrani

Sant' Andrea Cathedral, Amalfi

Sunrise between Amalfi and Atrani

Ravello has an enviable ridge-top location

Door at Sant' Andrea Cathedral, Amalfi

To the west of Amalfi the Via Maestra dei Villaggi, an old mule track that dates from the ninth century, leads through lemon groves and idyllic villages far from the tourist trail. Matriarchs returning from local markets patiently and steadily climb the endless steps back to their homes. Mules are still used to transport goods between the main roads and villages, and goat herders run their animals along the track to pastures new.

The most famous walking trail along the Amalfi coast is the fancifully named Footpath of the Gods (Sentiero degli Dei). Running from the mountain village of Bomerano, it snakes its way high up along the coastal cliffs to the village of Nocelle, from where there is a popular trail extension down to the seaside town of Positano. It is an outstanding walk, not simply because the views of the Mediterranean coastline and the island of Capri are majestic, but also because it is relatively easygoing as it descends gradually the entire way. From Bomerano, the footpath skirts around terraced lemon groves and ancient, ruined mountain huts, and above thrilling drops down to Praiano at the foot of the steep, forested slopes below. From Nocelle, a short section along a quiet mountain road leads to the village of Montepertuso and on towards a lengthy, knee-pounding set of steps that takes you all the way down to Positano.

Picturesque, with pastel-coloured houses that seem to be almost stacked on top of each other as they climb up the steep cliff walls, Positano arcs around a small beach and cove. A powerful centre of trade during the twelfth century, the town then fell from grace. Today, it is packed with chic Italian stores and boutique hotels – during the busier seasons visitors fill the narrow streets and it can be a struggle to walk around. For many people, Positano is the only taste they get of this stunning coastline, but by wandering the Amalfi coast's trails and passageways you will discover that the ancient character of the region remains intact.

ⓘ

Although it is possible to walk year-round on the Amalfi coast, from late June through August the high temperatures are probably too extreme for most people. The nearest international airport is Naples, from where it is a two- to three-hour journey by a combination of bus and train or taxi to Amalfi. There is an excellent SITA bus network for getting around the coastal villages and towns. Hiring a car is not necessary. Parking space is severely restricted around the towns on the coast, another good reason to use the buses. Julian Tippett's excellent walking guidebook, *Landscapes of Sorrento, Amalfi and Capri – Car Tours and Walks* by Julian Tippett (Sunflower), gives detailed descriptions and maps of many of the possible walks.

Footpath of the Gods, near Bomerano

The Footpath of the Gods descends gently to Nocelle

The Routeburn Track
New Zealand

Spring blossom, Te Anau

Moss-laden forest, Routeburn Valley

Key Summit

The mountains are big, the valleys broad and waterfalls tumble and rumble at almost every corner. Often hailed as one of the world's best walks, the Routeburn Track is an enduring New Zealand classic.

This 38-km trek leads through a pristine mountain landscape, the heartland of the Southern Alps, and, thanks to a well laid-out track that traverses rather than ascends the lofty surrounding peaks, it is accessible to anyone with a pair of hiking boots and a sense of adventure. The three-day route wanders between Fiordland National Park and Mount Aspiring National Park, following the Hollyford Valley before

swinging east into the Dart Valley. Along the way the Ailsa, Humboldt and Darran mountain ranges tower majestically above the trail.

People have been exploring this vast landscape for centuries. Maoris were the first to come here, looking for greenstone, the highly prized New Zealand jade. In their pursuit of rich supplies they forged a passage that connected the key sources of this stone – in the Dart Valley in the east and along the Arahura river on the west coast – and established a blueprint for part of today's path. However, it wasn't until the 1930s that the track became fully established as a 'tramping route', the New Zealand term for a hiking trail.

Key Summit nature trail

Lake Marion, Key Summit

The trek begins at the divide just off the Milford-to-Te Anau road. Cloaking forest shrouds the first 3 km of the path, as arching trees, dripping with goblin moss, almost prevent any mountain views. As you climb steadily you may catch a flash of yellow from the endangered mohua or yellowhead bush canary; found only on South Island it is sometimes spotted here.

After about an hour's walking the dense vegetation becomes more sparse and the sweeping depths of the Hollyford Valley are gradually revealed below. Backpacks can be temporarily cast off and left at a signpost marking a side path, and a series of easy switchbacks takes you above the treeline and on to Key Summit. This lofty vantage point was named by its first European visitors, David McKellar and George Gunn, who mapped this section of the route in 1861, and is a memorable viewpoint on the route. As you emerge from the trees an all-surrounding vista of peaks greets you – a panorama on an epic scale. Wooden boardwalks wind around to a viewpoint over Lake Marion and the mountain slopes are so densely forested they look as though they have been wrapped in green velvet.

After returning to the main path you descend to the tranquil waters of Lake Howden. Here a shingle shore is a great spot for lunch, with views leading towards the Greenstone Saddle to the south and the Capples Track to the west. The next water you see, 3 km further on, is the frothing plumes of Earland Falls, an 80-metre cascade. The overhanging canopy thins to reveal this soaring highlight. As the water ricochets off the surrounding boulders the spray offers an uplifting moment of refreshment.

The track then eases gently along through more lush forest to reach the Orchard, a clearing from which you can see the grand and often snow-capped summit of 2502-metre Mount Christina. The route then descends to the Mackenzie Hut, your overnight stop.

After a night's rest and a shower you will be ready for the second day's walk. This section of the trail begins by gently skirting the nearby

Earland Falls

Early morning reflections, Lake Mackenzie

Routeburn Valley

boulder-fringed Lake Mackenzie then winds through a magical moss-laden forest. As the woodland clears, an upward stretch of zigzagging path emerges. Far less arduous than it looks from below, it climbs to the resplendent Ocean Peak Corner. As you swing around this rocky bend the next striking panorama makes a showcase appearance. Below, the Hollyford Valley stretches northwards to views of the Tasman Sea while to the west the towering Darran Mountains soar skywards. The path then takes a lofty traverse along the Hollyford

Beech forest, Routeburn Valley

View over Lake Mackenzie en route to Ocean Peak Corner

Lake Harris

Face, which gives you plenty of time to absorb the wonder of this wild mountain passageway, and to catch a glimpse of Mount Tutoko, at 2723 metres the highest peak in Fiordland.

The highest point of the trail itself is at Harris Saddle, which at only 1300 metres seems surprisingly low. And this is perhaps why the Routeburn Track is so special. It is a walkway through a wild, untouched landscape and takes walkers into the mountains but does not require them to scale any great heights.

Dramatic mountain vistas are all around you as the path climbs gently around Lake Harris with its dazzling deep-blue waters. Bordered at one end by the Valley of the Trolls, a sublime rock-filled gorge, the southern end opens out into the upper reaches of the Routeburn Valley and here the path weaves a sharp descent. This can definitely make your legs feel they are working – but the open

Darran Mountain Range

Dart river

mountain valley with its huge glacial boulders, burbling streams and grassy knolls will entice you to linger. The day ends with the grand finale of the Routeburn Falls, a series of jagged, stepped waterfalls, alongside which your lodging for the night is spectacularly perched.

From a rocky, tree-fringed bluff outside the lodge, you can see what is to come on the final day's walk. Like a snaking conga line, the Routeburn river twists its way along the valley floor. An hour's tramp through rich, mixed beech forest brings you to the open expanse of the Routeburn Flats, over which resplendent Mount Xenicus stands guard. For 4 km the route follows the sparkling turquoise waters of the Routeburn river, and swaying suspension bridges take you across tumbling streams. The road head that signals the end of the walk is a further 9 km on – and may well come all too soon.

Swing bridge over the Routeburn river

ⓘ

Air New Zealand has several flights daily into Queenstown, the nearest airport for the Routeburn Track. There are two options for walking the track. One is as a 'freedom walker', carrying your own equipment and staying at designated Department of Conservation huts and campsites. Alternatively, guided treks with fully catered lodges are offered by Ultimate Hikes, which can also provide equipment such as rucksacks and raincoats. The trekking season runs from November to late April.

Dusk at Rowardennan, Loch Lomond

West Highland Way
Scotland

Descending from Conic Hill towards Loch Lomond

From the soft pastoral Lowlands to the majestic mountains of the north, the West Highland Way offers history, heritage and a chance to walk through the heart of the Highlands. Stretching for 152 km, it cuts a route from the outskirts of Scotland's biggest city, along the shores of its largest freshwater loch and across one of its wildest moors before ultimately arriving at the foot of its highest mountain: Ben Nevis.

Officially opened in 1980, the West Highland Way is Scotland's first long-distance walking route. It is based on much older routes, such as the eighteenth-century military roads constructed by England's General Wade and the long-established drovers' roads used to herd livestock to the richer markets of the Lowlands, as well as the more modern railway tracks that now lie abandoned.

Over 50,000 walkers embark on this journey every year, and most commonly they start in the south. Ten minutes by train from Glasgow is Milngavie, pronounced 'Mullguy', where a granite obelisk marks the beginning of the trail. From here the path roughly follows meandering Allander Water to the edge of Mugdock Wood and continues on past Craigallian Loch backed by the distinctive mound-shaped hill of Dumgoyach. Very quickly, the urban landscape fades away.

After a short section on the grassy track known as Tinkers Loan, you climb a stile and get a glimpse of things to come: the terraced Campsie Fells, the rough escarpment of the Strathblane Hills and the knobbly mass of Dumgoyne rear ahead. As though on an invisible threshold, you sense you are about to enter a wilder landscape.

This feeling is reinforced the following day as the path crosses wide, gorge-fringed moorland and climbs steadily to the top of 361-metre Conic Hill. From the summit Loch Lomond stretches out below and lofty mountain tops, including Ben Vorlich, Ben Vane and the Luss Hills, reach skywards. Mountain and water meet and merge. This is the Highlands.

Queen Elizabeth Forest Park

The view also takes in a distinctive string of islands in the loch. These are part of the Highland Boundary fault, which runs 260 km from Arran in the west to Stonehaven on Scotland's east coast and marks a clear separation between Highland and Lowland. From here

Evening storm clouds gather over Balmaha, Loch Lomond

The Bridge of Orchy

the route passes through the heart of the Highlands, where granite mountains are rarely far away.

After descending Conic Hill, the path largely follows the banks of Loch Lomond, winding through re-established native woodland, and across rocky coves and beaches dotted with gnarled trees. Just before the village of Rowardennan the summit of Ben Lomond, the most southerly of Scotland's Munros – peaks at least 914 metres high – comes into view.

Loch Tulla, seen on the descent from the Bridge of Orchy

A deep sense of history pervades the route. As it continues along the heavily wooded lochside it passes Rob Roy's Cave, said to be a hideaway of the Highland hero. A cattle dealer and the son of a clan chieftain, he became an outlaw when he failed to pay back money he had borrowed from the Duke of Montrose – the duke put a price on his head and Rob Roy's life on the run began.

The route leads to Inverarnan where, close by, you will find the West Highland Way's oldest pub: the Drovers Inn. It has been serving travellers for three centuries and Rob Roy, Robert Louis Stevenson, James Boswell and Robert Burns, the nation's bard, are all believed to have been customers. With its leather-bound books, a claymore strung on the wall, smoke-blackened interior and flickering candlelight, the inn is redolent of a bygone era.

While the landscape now offers walkers tranquillity, the region was once rife with conflict. There were violent raids to steal livestock and clans jostled for territory. After Loch Lomond the route is rarely far from General Wade's military roads, the remains of his efforts to link the Lowlands and Fort William in the eighteenth century when the English came to Scotland to bring the Highlands under their control. As the route penetrates further north it is easy to see why the troops felt threatened by this vast and desolate landscape – when you leave the village of Tyndrum the sweeping valley overlooked by the grand bulge of Beinn Odhar is as forbidding today as it must have been to the soldiers who marched along the still visible cobbled road.

The sturdy, high-arched Bridge of Orchy leads onwards to Loch Tulla and Rannoch Moor. This is the wildest and most remote section of the walk, dominated by small, lonely lochans and dark peat bogs. The route descends to the head of the dramatic and infamous Glen Coe, where the bloody massacre of the MacDonald clan by the Campbells took place in 1692. The grand pyramidal mass of Buachaille Etive peak is positioned like a sentry at the entrance.

The West Highland Way climbs out of the glen via the Devil's Staircase, so called by the soldiers who had to carve out this zigzagging route. The ascent is far easier than the name suggests, as the path gradually weaves to a pass at 548 metres. The descent down the rugged mountainside leads to the village of Kinlochleven.

The final section climbs through birch woods that give way to views over Loch Leven. Remnants of the past remain in the shape of abandoned farms, such as Tigh-na-steubhaich, a rambling ruin in the lonely pass of Lairigmòr. The trail now dips and turns through conifer plantations until it finally drops into Glen Nevis and journey's end in the town of Fort William.

Depending on the weather, this final section may just tease you with lofty mountain views of Ben Nevis. And if there is strength in your legs, you may well be tempted to reach one final summit.

ⓘ

The walk along the West Highland Way is generally spread across six or seven days, but this can be extended to ten days. The busiest times are the summer months when advance booking of accommodation is recommended. Weather-wise the best months can be May and September. Macs Adventure specializes in providing both guided and self-guided trips, and will handle all accommodation booking. They will arrange baggage transfers between accommodation each day, allowing you to keep your day's load to the essential minimum. They can also organize private transfers back to Glasgow once you have finished the walk. Alternatively, rail and coach services depart from Fort William daily.

Stormy evening light at Loch Tulla

Loch Leven, Kinlochleven

Sunrise breaks over a lochan on Rannoch Moor

Sakura at Nanzen-ji Temple

There is no better way to delve into the ancient, eastern spirit of Kyoto, Japan's majestic, imperial capital, than strolling around the city's exquisite Buddhist temples and shrines. If you venture there during springtime, you may catch the very brief sakura season when the cherry-blossom trees bloom, lining the footpaths with an extravaganza of ephemeral floral beauty.

Situated about 370 km southwest of Tokyo on the island of Honshu, in a narrow waist of land between the Sea of Japan and the Pacific Ocean, Kyoto – originally known as Heiankyo, or 'capital of peace' – is extraordinarily well preserved. For over 1000 years, from the end of the eighth century, it was the imperial, religious and intellectual capital of Japan. Although it lost its political power to Tokyo in 1868, it has remained a major centre and almost 2000 Buddhist temples and Shinto shrines testify to its continuing role at the heart of Japanese religion.

Temples of Kyoto

Japan

Osawanoike Pond at Daikaku-ji Temple

The temple walks are spread around the cardinal points of the compass, and it is worth spending a day or two exploring each direction. In the east lies one of the city's most popular walking trails, the Philosopher's Path, which runs from Ginkaku-ji Temple to Nanzen-ji Temple along a beautiful waterway lined with cherry-blossom trees. The path, named for the renowned Kyoto philosopher Nishida Kitarô, who used to frequent it, is a hugely popular place to witness the ethereal, white and pink sakura blossoms making their brief appearance. Within two weeks at most, the spring rains and wind send the delicate flowers falling gently to the ground.

Zen garden at Ginkaku-ji Temple

Cherry blossom on the Philosopher's Path

The Zen temple of Ginkaku-ji was originally built as a villa by the Muromachi shogun Ashikaga Yoshimasa in 1482. Twirled around a small stream and several ponds at the foot of a wooded, mossy hill, the temple complex has a large Zen garden of carefully swept, light grey stones, arranged in dynamic stripes, and a perfectly sculpted mound. Nanzen-ji Temple, at the path's southern end, is entered through a mammoth Sanmon gate. Established in 1291 by the emperor Kameyama, it is the headquarters of the Rinzai school of Zen and one of the most important Zen Buddhist temples in the world. With its stunning location, at the base of the forested Higashiyama Hills, it is a

Temple slippers at Fushimi Inari Taisha shrine

Gravel mound at Ginkaku-ji Temple

fitting finale to the Philosopher's Path. The vast and peaceful Maruyama Park, where the cherry-blossom displays are exceptional, is a short stroll southwest from Nanzen-ji.

A five-minute train ride to the south of Kyoto takes you to one of the city's most iconic shrines, Fushimi Inari Taisha; a wonderful place to spend half a day exploring the unique trails around the hillside grounds. The shrine boasts thousands of torii gates, which are erected so close together that they create surreal, brilliant orange and vermilion tunnels around the footpaths. Inari is the Shinto god of rice and the numerous fox figures around the site represent his messengers. Relatively few people venture out on to the paths furthest from the main shrine, where a tree-shrouded lake and bamboo trees await.

Some of Kyoto's most enchanting temples are to the west of the city in the Arashiyama Hills. An excellent half-day walk takes you from Tenryu-ji Temple, with its ornate gardens, to Seiryo-ji Temple in

Lake at Fushimi Inari Taisha shrine

Tunnels of torii gates line the trails at Fushimi Inari Taisha shrine

the beautifully preserved, tranquil district of Sagano. From Saga-Arashiyama station, a 40-minute rail journey from Kyoto, it is a brief walk to Tenryu-ji, the 'temple of the heavenly dragon'. Established in 1339, its halls and temples are linked by raised wooden boardwalks. Adjoining it is the exquisite Sogen Garden, one of the oldest Zen gardens in Japan. En route to Seiryo-ji Temple, it is possible to take a stroll through a giant bamboo forest and visit several other temples, including Nison-in, where maple trees are an impressive sight during autumn. From Seiryo-ji, the walk can be extended by a couple of kilometres or take a short taxi ride to the beautiful Daikaku-ji Temple, set around the idyllic Osawanoike Pond. It is off the beaten tourist track but much favoured by local people.

Foxes are regarded as messengers in Shinto

Just to the northwest of the centre of Kyoto are two of the city's most popular temples: Kinkaku-ji – the Golden Pavilion – and Ryoan-ji with its strikingly simple Zen rock garden. Be warned, though, you will be hard-pressed to find a Zen-like peace at either, as both temples are constantly overcrowded with tour-bus groups. A little further west, and easily reachable on foot from Ryoan-ji, is Daitoku-ji Temple. Accessed via another impressive Sanmon wooden gate and broad steps, the open spaces of its main courtyard will be a welcome relief.

Previous pages: Giant bamboo forest near Seiryo-ji Temple in Arashiyama district

Garden at Sanzen-in Temple

Venture further from the city to the surrounding countryside and you get a taste of what Kyoto was like in bygone times. At Ohara, about a one-hour bus ride north, the pace of life drops considerably and the enchanting, ancient temple at Sanzen-in is a mossy, green paradise of calm. Rarely visited by tourists, it is a hidden gem with beautiful, wooded gardens ripe for exploring on foot. Half-emerging from the lawns are beguiling, tiny stone figures with childlike, innocent faces, which cannot help but bring a perfect Zen moment of unbridled joy.

Many airlines, including ANA, offer international flights into Tokyo, from where it is a thrilling two-and-a-half hour Shinkansen (bullet train) journey to Kyoto. The Japan National Tourist Organization can supply a wide range of information on visiting Kyoto and the temples, including an excellent brochure of walking routes. It can also advise on the availability of volunteer student guides, who ease the way if you don't speak Japanese. There is an excellent and cheap system of buses and metro trains for getting around Kyoto and its environs. Taxis often take far longer because of heavy traffic. The sakura season shifts from year to year but generally arrives in Kyoto in late March or early April. Autumn is also a beautiful time to visit the city.

Lake at Sanzen-in Temple

Lofoten Islands
Norway

Dawn light over the Arctic Ocean, near Mortsund

Roughly hewn granite spires, isolated fjords and often tempestuous seas, all swathed in the ethereal light of the midnight sun, help make the Lofoten Islands one of Mother Nature's most exhilarating and dramatic creations. Lying off the northwest coast of Norway, well within the Arctic Circle, they offer a multitude of uncrowded walking trails among some of the most spectacular scenery to be found on the planet.

The Lofoten chain consists of four main islands, Austvågøy, Vestvågøy, Flakstadøy and Moskenesøy, and two outlying ones, Værøy and Røst. Shaped like a crecent moon, the archipelago arcs over 200 km into the blue-green waters of the Norwegian Sea. Thanks to the Gulf

Fishing trawler in the bay at Eggum at midnight

Rorbu at Nusfjord

Stream, despite being inside the Arctic Circle the islands enjoy an exceptionally mild climate for their latitude with temperatures even in the depth of winter rarely dropping much below zero Celsius.

An experience not to be missed is a stay in a rorbu (a traditional fisherman's cottage). First built in around the twelfth century as cheap accommodation to cope with the seasonal influx of fishermen, many rorbu, such as those at Mortsund, near Leknes on Vestvågøy, have been converted into comfortable cabins for visitors. Set at the water's edge, sometimes on stilts, one of these ochre-red, clapboard huts makes a homely base from which to explore. The peak of Heia, which rises just behind those at Mortsund, is ideal for a first, short walk to get an

expansive view over the tranquil waters and rocky islets of Buknesfjorden, and southwestwards along the headlands of the Lofoten chain.

While all the main islands offer excellent walking opportunities, the ones at the southwestern end of the group are perhaps the most alluring. The opportunity to walk in the light of the midnight sun is one of the Lofoten Islands' major attractions, and several places along the outside edge of the chain make for good vantage points. One of the most beautiful trails runs along the shoreline from Eggum to Unstad, on Vestvågøy.

A small collection of yellow, red, white and blue wooden houses, the village of Eggum seems to be trapped between the sea and the imposing, sheer cliffs of Mustaren peak. Shortly after leaving Eggum, the path passes by Head, a visual-illusion sculpture by the Swiss artist Markus Raetz. When you walk around it the head sculpture seems to flip upside down and several other face shapes appear. With no islands or any other land to get in the way to the northwest, there

Eggum village

Trail from Eggum to Unstad

Sea mist at Flakstadpollen fjord

Rorbu at Mortsund

Sea fog rolling around the peaks on Flakstadpollen fjord

is an uninterrupted view of the midnight sun along the trail. The soft, soothing light, imbued with endless subtle tones of yellow, pink, orange, blue and purple, rebounds from the cliffs.

Further south, to the west of Leknes, another short coastal walk follows an old gravel road from Haukland to Utakleiv, via white-sand beaches and the rocky headland at Tåa. Rarely seen by visitors, this area is a favourite with local people and one of the beaches, on Vikspollen bay, was recently voted the most beautiful in Norway.

If you could walk on only one the Lofoten Islands, few would argue that Flakstadøy is the best choice. The village of Flakstadpollen stands on an astounding fjord with a backdrop of towering, craggy mountains, where frequent sea fogs and mists are swirling protagonists in the often stunning evening-light displays. There are numerous high mountain routes around the fjord for more experienced hikers and a good choice of short walks, along the beaches and into the foothills, for those with less time or wilderness knowledge. Just to the west, the coastal trail from Ytresand to Mulstøa, an easy evening walk along the shoreline, is another ideal vantage point from which to watch the midnight sun.

Fishing trawler at Mortsund

Ethereal midnight light near Eggum

At the southern end of Flakstadøy a more challenging coast path, which makes for a good half-day walk, leads from the tiny village of Nesland to Nusfjord, a World Heritage Site widely touted as Norway's best-preserved fishing village. Tucked away from the open sea in the steep, grey-rock fjord, Nusfjord boasts an excellent museum trail through old fishing-related buildings, from boathouses to a saw

Morning light on a rorbu at Mortsund

mill. Drying cod skins hang from rorbu eaves, a raised boardwalk takes you round the natural harbour and there are coffee shops to replenish energy supplies for the return walk.

No walking trip to the Lofoten Islands would be complete without accessing the high mountains that dominate so much of the landscape. Just before Moskenesøy's main E10 road runs out abruptly at the succinctly named village of Å, an outstanding, though strenuous, trail leads from the village of Sørvågen up to the mountain hut at Munkebu. It traverses below a thundering waterfall to reach Stuvdalsvatnet Lake, where a spattering of fishing huts line the shore. After rounding the lake the hard work begins, with fixed handrail chains to aid your passage as the route ascends a steep, rocky ridge.

At the top of the climb, the views stretch across silvery-blue hanging glaciers and high mountain lakes in steep-backed cirques.

To the east, the ridge drops sharply away down into Djupfjorden and out to the wide expanse of Vestfjorden, which separates the Lofoten Islands from the mainland. Far below, fishing trawlers head out from port, while ahead lies the Munkebu hut. When you sit on its veranda, the silence of the mountains will envelop you.

ⓘ
Inntravel offers flexible self-guided walking trips to the Lofoten Islands, including car hire with Hertz and comprehensive hiking maps and directions. SAS fly into Norway's capital, Oslo, and from Oslo further north to Bodo. From Bodo, it is just a 20-minute flight with Widerøe to Leknes on Vestvågøy island. Statles Rorbusenter in Mortsund offers rorbu accommodation with modern comforts. There is a reasonable bus service on the islands, but if you want maximum flexibility to explore hiring a car is the way to get around.

Morne Trois Pitons

Dominica

The Caribbean conjures up images of white sandy beaches, luxury resorts, relaxation and overdressed cocktails, but Dominica is different, very different. With merely a handful of volcanic black-sand beaches, one five-star hotel and pristine rainforests perfect for action-packed hiking, only cocktails survive the comparison. After tackling the best trails the Caribbean has to offer, those fancy drinks will taste sweeter than ever.

Nestled between Guadeloupe and Martinique, about halfway along the crescent-moon-shaped chain of the Lesser Antilles, Dominica is the Caribbean island that progress left behind. With no direct international flights, getting there requires a modicum of effort, which thankfully is enough to deter the tourist masses. Even the cruise ships that stop by every now and then rarely stay overnight. This relative isolation combined with a progressive government initiative to protect natural parts of the island, as reserves and national parks, means Dominica is more authentically Caribbean than almost any other island in the region: tranquil, green and as easy-paced as a lazy Sunday morning.

Nearing the island, the view from the plane window is of precipitous valleys, heavily cloaked in steaming, impenetrable

Middleham Falls

Boiling Lake

Thermal stream, near Roseau

rainforest leading up to the ragged, dark peaks of Morne Trois Pitons National Park. Such is the immediate allure and mystery of the place, it is easy to understand why the *Pirates of the Caribbean* movies were filmed on the island.

One of the appeals of hiking on Dominica is that your days don't have to be all about walking. Up in the foothills behind Roseau, the capital, there are spectacular, natural hot springs with massage treatments and holistic healing on tap to ease your mind and soothe those weary feet and shoulders. Fruit and vegetables, which have probably been grown within a stone's throw of the restaurant table, are so succulent and tasty they stir memories of how food used to taste before global markets became the norm. Hummingbirds flit skilfully among vibrantly green broad leaves looking for nectar, lizards scurry across the soft, moist ground and the humid warmth wraps itself around you like a comfort blanket. In Dominica, everything feels right with the world.

Contrary to first impressions, the intimidating terrain of Morne Trois Pitons National Park, which covers around 6880 hectares, offers a range of excellent walks to suit just about any ability. One of the easier options, and a good choice for initially stretching your legs, is the two- to three-hour return hike up to Middleham Falls. The trail winds its way through dense rainforest, barely giving a hint of the powerful cascade ahead. After an hour or so, the increasing roar heralds your arrival and soon after a blanket of fine spray drenches everything. The 60-metre fall plummets from a small cleft among the trees and, barely touching a rock en route, splashes into the large, green plunge pool far below.

Morne Trois Pitons, after which the national park is named, is the island's second-highest mountain, and there is no gentle warm-up if you decide to hike to its summit. From the start the route follows steep and often slippery steps and muddy paths – compensated for by great views over the entire eastern side of the island.

Exotic flowers are found all over the island

A bizarre twist comes near the summit, where the trail winds its way among and through a dense tangle of giant tree roots: a dark, dank and utterly fascinating underworld. Then, with little warning, you pop your head out of a gap and find you are at the top – a unique approach to a summit. The views over much of the island and out to the Caribbean Sea are outstanding.

Tangled rhododendron roots near the summit of Morne Trois Pitons

The most renowned trail on Dominica, and quite possibly the best trek in the entire Caribbean, takes in pristine wilderness and surreal geothermal areas on the way to Boiling Lake. Although it is only a six- to seven-hour return hike, it is not for the faint hearted. The trail starts out easily enough, easing its way gently upwards through thick rain-forest from dramatic Titou Gorge, where early returners may get a chance to cool off with a swim.

After crossing Trois Pitons river, tagged Breakfast river by the guides and the only accessible place to drink refreshingly chilled

Descent into the Valley of Desolation

Roseau Bay

rainforest water, the trail climbs steeply and incessantly up the flank of Morne Nichols on to a breathtaking knife-edge ridge. All around, lush green tree tops rise and fall with valleys that few people have seen at ground level. After cresting the ridge, where blustery weather conditions can exaggerate the effects of exposure, the trail takes a hair-raising dive into the spectacular Valley of Desolation. Near the bottom there is the first whiff of sulphur, and wispy puffs of steam from the geothermal springs can be seen.

As the trail descends into the steam, the valley floor sparks into life, bubbling and hissing as you pass fumaroles and mud pots. Beyond the springs, the trail constricts and continues high above the sulphur-filled waters of a stream, before a stiff climb leads up to the dramatically located Boiling Lake.

Set deep in a steep-sided mountain bowl, backdropped by soaring green peaks, the milky-blue lake boils and threatens to erupt into something much bigger but never does. The size of the lake has fluctuated drastically over time and it has even drained away completely before refilling itself, sometimes with cold water that slowly comes back to the boil. It is a wondrous and wild sight on this idyllic island, and it makes the ascent back out of the Valley of Desolation seem fully worth it.

ⓘ

The Dominica Tourist Office can supply information about all aspects of visiting the island and walking there, including recommending local guides. There are no direct international flights, so it is necessary to reach Dominica via Antigua or one of the other nearby Caribbean islands. British Airways offers direct flights to Antigua and other Caribbean destinations. There is a wide range of accommodation on offer, from seafront hotels in Roseau to spa retreats in the hills above.

Goatherd Leap (Salto del Cabrero)

Drovers' Roads
Andalucia, Spain

Step on to the drovers' roads of Andalucia and you will find yourself walking through a way of life that has defined the landscape for centuries. These well-trodden routes are the natural corridors used by shepherd, muleteer and goat herder alike. Thankfully, today you don't need a herd to explore them.

Whitewashed village of Grazalema

The roads can be found throughout Andalucia – the alluring deep south of Spain and heartland of flamenco, sherry and the grand sierras. The region is famous for its pueblos blancos (white villages) and one of them, Grazalema, is among the many places from which drovers used to depart.

Located in the northwest and a two-hour drive from Malaga, in a high valley in the Sierra del Endrinal, it clusters beneath the dominating rocky mass of Peñón Grande in the heart of Andalucia's first designated natural park: Sierra de Grazalema. The village itself is a twist of cobbled streets, where colourful flowers tumble from window pots; the high sierras rear above the houses and verdant valleys trail below them. This is one of Spain's most ecologically outstanding

regions. Rare griffon vultures soar on warm thermals and over 30 different species of orchid as well as unique Pinsapo fir trees can be found.

A twist of different paths, worn into the landscape after years of use by sheep, goats and mules, lead from Grazalema to surrounding villages like lofty Zahara de la Sierra, roughly five hours' walk away, with its Moorish castle precariously seated atop a craggy cliffside. The fortress is one of the area's most distinctive sights with the

Embalse de Zahara, a vast man-made lake, near Zahara de la Sierra

Late afternoon light in the streets of Grazalema

whitewashed houses beneath it spilling out to offer ringside views over the brilliant azure waters of the lake, Embalse de Zahara. Close by, Goatherd Leap (Salto del Cabrero) preserves the legend of the broken-hearted herder who flung himself from the 80-metre high walls of the chasm.

An ideal walk through this pastoral landscape links Grazalema to the neighbouring village of Montejaque, 17 km away. The rough, cobbled track of the Camino Medieval [medieval road] skirts out of town beneath towering limestone cliffs. The tinkling of a lead goat's bell may still be heard, an echo of both past and present as the path remains a working route, still used by modern-day herders.

The route goes south through rolling grassland then weaves through the corkwoods. Here, harvested trees reveal glowing orange trunks where strips of cork have been freshly cut. The path emerges from the dense woods into a clearing known locally as the cork patio.

The lofty village of Zahara de la Sierra

Below, lush, open plains, speckled with plump, rounded tree tops, hum with birdsong and the occasional buzz of a dragonfly. It was here that the drovers would put their animals out to graze for a while. It is not hard to imagine them stopping beneath the shady bowers of a tree for a brief respite from the midday sun.

While journeys between villages could sometimes be long, and may even have required drovers to camp out overnight, huddled down

Tumbling wildflowers and packhorse bridges are typical of Andalucia

Wild iris

at the nearest watering hole, they were not always lonely. The roads they travelled on were the natural highways, busy routes that followed valleys and streams, and avoided mountain ascents. They were the only way to get to market.

The main trail continues roughly northeastwards, towards what was once a bustling *finca* (farm) and is now a ramshackle ruin. The remains of the stone threshing floor can be found among the jumble of grasses and wild flowers, a hint of what were very different times.

Further down the track, orderly lines of olive trees cut stripes across the hillside and the rich brown earth glows with reddish hues in the afternoon light. The route now winds its way through the groves, a sign once more of the continuing relationship between the fertile land and its people; another crop carefully tended to produce an annual harvest.

Wild flowers scatter the banks, a confused sea of colours with yellows and pinks lapping at its edges. The track climbs a little higher towards a rocky pass amid the towering Sierra de Montalate. The limestone rock has been carved into deep notches and rough boulders, which line the drovers' route as it heads towards the valley floor. Up here in the peaceful solitude, the distant buzz of machinery

Flower box window, Grazalema

Evening stroll around the streets of Benaocaz

Ancient threshing floor on the Montejaque drovers' road

Various drovers' roads lead through Sierra de Grazalema National Park

from the sheep farm below is the only clue that life has moved on in any way.

The route now contours gracefully along the valley edge, then curves its way downwards on a good path. Slowly Montejaque comes into view. Chickens scratch for seeds in the verges and a terrace of squat, stone cottages lines the road into the village, where old men gather in the cobbled streets to catch up on the day's events.

Dawn mist over an Andalucian farm

Sheep flocks on an ancient route to Grazalema

ⓘ

With the exception of the hot summer months, Andalucia has an ideal climate for walking. One of the best times to visit the region is during spring (May) when its wild flowers are abundant. The nearest international airport to Grazalema is Malaga, approximately a two-hour drive away. Andalucian Adventures provides guided walking tours throughout the region, with a specialist wild-flowers tour based in Grazalema. Their walking programme includes many opportunities to explore the drovers' roads in this area.

Boston's Freedom Trail
USA

Old and new mix easily in downtown Boston

Walking along Boston's Freedom Trail takes you deep into the historical roots of modern America. It was here that the seeds of the American Revolution were sown, and Paul Revere rode out from the city in 1775 to warn fellow militia leaders of the impending British attack.

Notched into the northern corner of Massachusetts Bay, on the northeast coast of the USA, Boston has retained much of its old architecture, with pastel-coloured clapboard houses and old cobbled streets that give it a distinctly European feel. Because it is relatively compact, getting around the city on foot is the easiest and most enjoyable way to get a taste of its revolutionary spirit.

Massachusetts State House, an icon of the city

Known affectionately nowadays as the 'cradle of liberty', Boston grew around the European colonists, primarily Puritans, who arrived in the New World in the mid-seventeenth century. Their loyalty to the British crown was severely strained over a number of years, leading to the revolution. In 1765 came the Stamp Act, which the colonists argued was unconstitutional – there should be 'no taxation without representation' – and which sparked riots in the city. Then, in 1773, a 3-cent tax was imposed on tea, which led to the Boston Tea Party when a shipment of tea was thrown into the harbour in protest.

Freedom Trail marker

By 1775, relations between the colonists and the British were at crisis point. The continuing interference from Britain was met with

The USS *Constitution* helped defeat Britain in 1812

increasing resistance and the Americans had begun to mobilize and train as Minutemen – members of the militia who were ready to fight at a minute's notice. On 18 April, British troops moved to attack Lexington, a nearby patriot stronghold. Paul Revere arranged for two warning lanterns to be hung in the tower of Old North Church, then rode at night to alert the Minutemen. The next morning the battle began.

Although you can walk the 4.8-km Freedom Trail in either direction, the acknowledged starting point is Boston Common, America's oldest

Boston city from the top of Bunker Hill monument

Moorings on Charles river

public park. Opposite the common stands the golden-domed Massachusetts State House. In 1795 Paul Revere and Samuel Adams, a fellow patriot and by then state governor, laid the cornerstone for the building. Today, its glittering, gilded roof is an icon of the city.

The trail descends gently past Park Street Church to the Granary Burying Ground, where several of the Sons of Liberty, the main protagonists in the American Revolution, are buried: as well as Samuel Adams and Paul Revere they include John Hancock, the first person to sign the Declaration of Independence. Further along

Tremont Street you pass King's Chapel with its high-sided box pews before turning on to School Street and passing the Old City Hall. Outside the hall, a statue of Benjamin Franklin celebrates Boston's favourite son and one of the founding fathers of modern America. He was a pupil at the Boston Latin School, which once stood on the site.

Boston was a literary mecca in the nineteenth century and the Old Corner Book Store, a charming brick building, used to house Ticknor & Fields, publishers of some of America's greatest writers, including Longfellow and Thoreau. Incongruously, it is now a jewellery shop. Opposite is one of the hubs of the revolution: the Old South Meeting House. The Sons of Liberty held many protest gatherings here in the run-up to the revolution, and it was here that Samuel Adams sparked the Boston Tea Party on 16 December 1773. He signalled the gathered protesters to head for the wharves to empty three British ships of their loads. By morning, almost 45 tons of tea were swilling around Boston harbour. The fuse to conflict was well and truly lit.

The most endearing building along the entire walk is the Old State House with its ornate tower of columns and rearing unicorns. The small, red-brick building's charm is enhanced by the looming glass

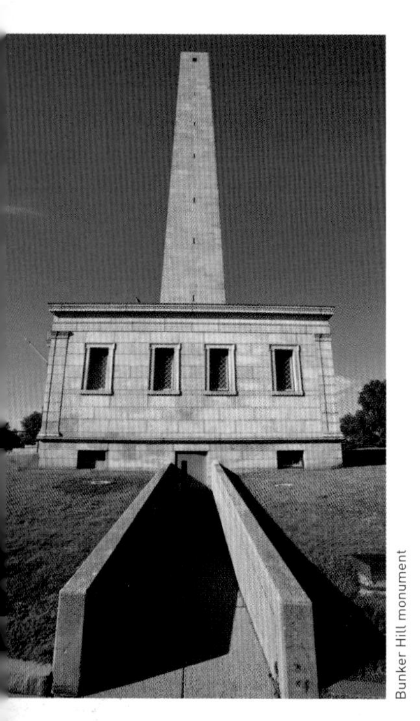
Bunker Hill monument

Freedom Trail end point at Bunker Hill

The Old State House, dwarfed by modern skyscrapers

Traditional clapboard houses near Bunker Hill

skyscrapers all around it. Used as a meeting house by America's British rulers, it was a focus of patriot grievances and the scene of the Boston Massacre in 1770, when rising tensions between the colonists and Britain led to brawls and five civilians were shot by British soldiers. Suitably, it was from its balcony in July 1776 that the Declaration of Independence was read aloud to rejoicing crowds below.

Past Fanueil Hall, heralded by a statue of Samuel Adams, his arms defiantly folded, the route passes through a narrow, cobbled street with original city pubs and Ye Olde Union Oyster House, which opened its doors in 1826 and is the city's oldest restaurant. It is little changed and a seat at the oyster bar is still much sought after.

The North End, with its countless Italian restaurants and cafés, was also home to Paul Revere; a visit to his lopsided, grey clapboard house, in North Square, gives an interesting insight into daily life in Boston's earliest days. On the tree-lined avenue to Old North Church, where the warning lanterns were hung, Revere is commemorated with a striking bronze statue depicting his horseback ride to warn of the impending British attack.

Across the broad, lazy Charles river, a favourite maritime playground for locals, is the Charlestown Navy Yard, home to the impressive tall ship, USS *Constitution*. From here, the trail leads to Bunker Hill. Three months after Paul Revere's midnight ride, the battle of Bunker Hill was under way. Today the hill is a lush green park, and it is here, at the top of a soaring monument with panoramic views over the harbour and city, that the Freedom Trail reaches its lofty and fitting climax. It may be only 4.8 km long, but it is a fascinating walk that takes you back through the birth of modern America.

ⓘ

The Freedom Trail is easy to navigate, thanks to frequent junction signs and a continuous red line along the pavement. It can be completed in a few hours, but you could just as easily spend a couple of days seeing all the places along the route. There is an information office at the starting point on Boston Common, with maps, books and details on guided tours – some with guides dressed in period costume. Hotel accommodation in the city centre can be fully booked and there are few budget options. The trail can be walked year-round, though winters can be hard in Boston.

Patriotism on show at a Bunker Hill fire station

On the trail in Charlestown

Tour du Mont Blanc

France, Italy and Switzerland

Trient village, Switzerland

Approaching Col de la Seigne, the gateway to Italy

Snow-capped mountains, lush meadows, wooded valleys, tumbling rivers and the tinkle of cowbells are the sights and sounds of this altogether Alpine experience. Taking in three different countries in roughly 14 days, the Tour du Mont Blanc (TMB) marches across the roof of western Europe, circling its most famous and highest peak.

Europe's most popular long-distance walk, with an estimated 10,000 hikers embarking on it each summer, the TMB was first undertaken in 1767 by Horace-Bénédict de Saussure. Some 170 km long, it winds in and out of valleys linked by a succession of high passes, following an

oval route around its grand mountain epicentre. Although there is an accumulated height gain and loss of roughly 10,000 metres, the highest pass is only 2665 metres, so no technical skills or equipment are needed to complete a circuit during the summer months.

The TMB can be walked in either a clockwise or anti-clockwise direction and there are a number of starting places. The traditional departure point is Les Houches in the Vallée de Chamonix.

A cable-car ride to Bellevue can short-cut the initial hard slog of the first day, after which there is plenty of climbing to be done on the steady ascent to the Col de Tricot at 2120 metres. A Nepalese-style

Torrent de Bionassay, on the trail in France

Alpine meadows ring to the sound of cowbells

suspension bridge that spans the turbulent waters of the Bionnassay must be crossed before the gradual climb upwards continues in earnest, past the sometimes rumbling Glacier de Bionnassay.

A series of switchbacks leads down to the clustered hamlet of Chalets de Miage, serenely positioned next to a burbling river bedecked with Alpine blooms. The path then climbs across the shoulder of Mont Truc before descending through deep green woodland to the pretty ski town of Les Contamines, your first overnight stop, where wood-fronted chalets line the high street.

The next day delivers another steady ascent that initially takes you along a paved mule track and rises through a striking hanging valley, which was formed by glacial erosion, to the Col du Bonhomme. The following lofty traverse to the Col de la Croix provides lengthy vistas of rolling mountain peaks. A popular descent option is to the Vallée des Glaciers and the tiny hamlet of Les Chapieux.

At the head of the valley is the Col de la Seigne; the gateway to Italy. At 2516 metres this pass offers the first potential view of mighty

Mont Blanc, set amidst the grand limestone slabs of the Pyramides Calcaires and the sweeping Vallon de la Lée Blanche. Further down, the pretty Rifugio Elizabetta nestles beneath the sweeping ice of Trélatête and Glacier de la Lée Blanche.

The next town is Cormayeur, where it is worth wandering down the high street if only to admire the chic style of its residents and savour a truly frothy cappuccino or a bowl of home-made pasta. The lush green Val Veni then leads into the Val Ferret, carrying the route onwards and gradually upwards to the 2537-metre Grand Col Ferret; take a backward glance here for the last sweeping views over Italy.

This is where you enter Switzerland and descend through typically rolling Alpine meadows. As you pass the barns and summer pastures of La Peula you will hear the unmistakable clatter of cow

Glacier de la Lée Blanche, Italy

Val Ferret, Italy

bells. Pretty wooden chalets, adorned with the vibrant red Swiss flag, dot the hillside as the path eventually winds into the small town of La Fouly. Set beneath the jutting, frozen cascade of the Glacier de l'A Neuve this is the obvious place for an overnight stay with a view.

Overlooking Champex, a village on the Swiss section of the TMB

The route then meanders enjoyably along the Swiss Val de Ferret, closely following its tumbling river, the Drance de Ferret, its banks lined with pink flowers. Later it slaloms through the chalets of Praz de Fort and the rustic farm buildings of Les Arlaches before ascending, through woodlands awash with wild mushrooms, to Champex. Set around a gracefully curved lake presided over by an intriguing modern sculpture of geese, this village is a popular base for walkers.

Val Ferret, Italy

Glacier de la Lée Blanche and Rifugio Elizabetta, Italy

Col du Bonhomme, France

Col de Tricot

La Breya, Switzerland

Aiguille du Midi overlooks Mont Blanc

A climb through ravined woods, across three different river beds, leads to the barns of Bovine and views down the Vallée du Rhône and to the distant Bernese Oberland mountains. At the 1526-metre Col de la Forclaz you can enjoy one of the local specialities, *tarte aux myrtilles* (blueberry tart), before an easy descent to the small village of Trient clustered around its church.

Vallée de Chamonix, seen from the Aiguille du Midi

From here it's a steady upwards pull to the Col de Balme, where the route crosses back into France and the grand U-shaped Vallée de Chamonix stretches ahead, separating the Aiguilles Rouges and the Mont Blanc massif. After the village of Argentière the path along the Grand Balcon offers airy views to the tumbling, crevasse-strewn Argentière glacier.

At the heart of the valley is the buzzing town of Chamonix, the Alpine capital of mountaineering, where climbers waiting for good weather drink coffee in pavement cafés and the towering mass of Mont Blanc is rarely out of sight. If you want to get even closer to the mountain, the Aiguille du Midi cable car glides upwards to a viewing platform at 3842 metres, from where the snowbound summit can be seen.

On the final section of the route some of the best views of Mont Blanc are from Le Brevant, before the path descends and winds its way through woodland back to Les Houches – making your circular tour of Europe's premier peak complete.

ⓘ

June to September, when most cable cars and the mountain huts are in service, are the most popular months for undertaking the Tour du Mont Blanc. There is no fixed way to walk the route, and accommodation can vary, from camps, mountain refuges to hotels or B&Bs in towns. Sherpa Expeditions offers a two-week escorted tour with hotel accommodation. Bags are transported daily, so you only have to carry a light daypack.

South West Coast Path

England

The coast path skirts the clifftops at Sennen

Waves exploding as they thunder on to rugged high cliffs, miles of sandy beaches and centuries of English and Celtic history await you on Britain's longest national walking trail: the South West Coast Path. Stretching for 1013 km from Minehead in the county of Somerset to Poole Harbour in Dorset, its countless access options and wide-ranging facilities en route give scope for everyone to experience one of Europe's most dramatic coastal landscapes.

Jutting out into the untameable expanses of the Atlantic Ocean, the southwest peninsula of Britain has been inhabited since around 10,000–11,000 BC, when it was in the grip of the last ice age. Nowadays, the warming currents of the North Atlantic Drift result in

First rays of light on Tintagel village

Sunset at Sennen

an exceptionally mild climate. Don't be fooled, though: mild may mean warm but it doesn't mean dry or calm. Storms are most frequent in autumn and winter, but be prepared for any weather at any time of the year.

The path was originally established in the early nineteenth century when the government employed coastguards to patrol the coastline, keeping watch for smugglers who used isolated beaches and coves to land goods and avoid import taxes.

Few people these days have the two months or so it would take to complete the entire route in one go. However, an advantage of this trail is that you can pick and mix where and how far you walk – save for a few isolated day-long sections, which are more committing, there are

Harbour at Port Issac

St Ives has inspired many painters and poets

Waves crash ashore at Sennen Cove

Celtic cross at St Materiana's Church

Ruined tin mine at Geevor

regular road-access points, villages and towns along the way. If you want to spend about a week sampling much of what the South West Coast Path offers, head for the north Cornwall sections between Tintagel Castle, the supposed birthplace of the legendary King Arthur, and Land's End, the most westerly point on the British mainland.

Perched atop a rocky promontory, Tintagel Castle would be beguiling even without its association with Arthur, whose historical role – and even his existence – today inspires more debate than ever. Now in ruins, it was built in the thirteenth century by Richard, Earl of Cornwall, but archaeologists have found evidence of human occupation dating back to the fifth century, the alleged time of Arthur. Its crumbling walls cling precariously to the steep, rugged slopes and it is easy to feel the spiritual attraction of such a dramatic natural location.

Surfing before Gull Rock at Trebarwith Strand

Pretty houses like this one line the streets of Port Issac

From the castle, the path climbs up to grassland above Glebe Cliff, to St Materiana's Church and the array of ancient Celtic stone crosses in its cemetery. The views out to sea, here as along the entire trail, are exceptional, especially around sunrise and sunset when the sky takes on an endless variety of moods, from stormy blazes of orange to gentle hues of pink and blue. Throughout the day, as the tides ebb and flow, waves crash on to vertical cliffs and the boulders below them, sending torrents of water leaping into the air. Few places feel so wild or so invigorating.

Past the old slate quarry at Lanterdan, the emerging hulk of Gull Rock offshore is an early herald of the path's descent to Trebarwith Strand, a huddle of shops and cafés just an hour or so away from Tintagel. It is a renowned surfing spot and, when the tide is out, boasts one of the best beaches in Cornwall with its long stretch of golden sand. For a good day's walk you can continue along the path as it climbs out of the valley and heads southwest towards Port Isaac, a pretty little village about 15 km from Tintagel that nestles at the head of a small inlet.

Fishing boats fill the harbour and the narrow, cobbled streets are lined with quaint stone cottages, some of which offer bed and breakfast.

An especially spectacular section of the South West Coast Path runs from St Ives, a tourist hot spot and home to the Tate St Ives art gallery, to Zennor Head three or four hours to the southwest. Leaving behind the buzz of popular Porthmeor Beach in St Ives, you are soon back in the wilds as you ascend to Hor Point. When you reach Zennor Head a short detour inland will lead you to Zennor itself. There you will find a delightful cluster of cottages around the Tinners Arms pub, the Norman church of St Senara and, in the village's grand old chapel, one of the best hostels on the trail.

From Zennor, the path skirts high above imposing dark cliffs to the whitewashed lighthouse at Pendeen Watch, a few hours away,

Trebarwith Strand is popular with surfers

Sennen Cove is renowned as one of Cornwall's best surf beaches

before continuing on past the Geevor tin mine, with its towering chimney stacks and ruined outbuildings – now an excellent museum. Tin mining in Cornwall declined after the mid-nineteenth century, but Geevor was still operating commercially right up until 1990. The precarious location of the mine workings and buildings at times defies belief and the land around this section of the trail is riddled with old shafts, so stick to the path.

Wreck of the RMS *Mulheim*, near Sennen Cove

Dramatic morning light at Tintagel

After a couple of hours you reach the chimney-topped promontory and old mine buildings at Cape Cornwall, once thought to be the furthest western point on the mainland. Land's End, its usurper, is now in sight, just 10 km further on. The path rolls across grassy slopes to take you to Sennen Cove, at the southern end of the wonderful sandy sweep of Whitesand Bay. This charming fishing village boasts possibly the best surf conditions in Cornwall – and has none of the hubbub and tourist paraphernalia that will greet you when you arrive at Land's End.

Stormy clouds at sunset near Sennen

Pendeen Watch lighthouse

Whichever way you choose to tackle this outstanding trail, the South West Coast Path will probably have you yearning for a two-month break to walk its entire length.

ⓘ

There is a wide range of accommodation along and near the trail, from campsites to B&Bs and hotels. The official South West Coast Path website has links to all the facilities en route, and a useful distance calculator for the sections of the path. Tides are notorious, so pick up a copy of the local tide tables and plan beach walks carefully to avoid getting cut off. If the winds are strong, it is wise to avoid the coast path all together. There are plenty of cosy, traditional pubs near by.

King Ludwig's Way
Germany

King Ludwig's Way skirts the foothills of the Alps near Wildsteig

Eccentric and colourful, Ludwig II ruled Bavaria for 22 years until his early death in 1886 – and left a legacy of fanciful castles as well as an enduring mystery about his demise. Walking King Ludwig's Way, a 120-km national trail, is a sumptuous week-long stroll through the landscapes and traditional culture that helped to shape him.

In the south of Germany, bordering the Alps, Bavaria is the country's largest region and also its wealthiest and most egalitarian. The trail begins at Leoni, near Starnberg, on the edge of the Starnbergsee, the

lake where the king met his death, and ends at Füssen, close to Ludwig's greatest masterpiece: the fairy-tale Neuschwanstein Castle.

The king's dreamy, peaceful character and his style of rule, which included extravagant building projects and substantial financial support for the composer Richard Wagner, caused unrest among his powerful political enemies. In 1886, with no solid medical evidence, he was declared insane and was deposed. Three days later, Ludwig went for a walk around the Starnbergsee with his physician, and later that night their bodies were found in the lake. Many theories, from

Farm fields en route to Wessobrun

Monastery at Wessobrun

suicide to murder, have been expounded to explain why they died, but the truth remains an intriguing mystery.

Although most daily sections of the trail involve about 20 km of walking, the first day's effort after arriving in Starnberg – a 90-minute train journey from Munich airport – is a gentle 7 km from Leoni back to Starnberg. You reach Leoni by cab or ferry, and the main reason for this loop is to visit the tiny Votiv Chapel on the lake shore, which was erected to commemorate Ludwig's death.

Next morning, you head from Starnberg towards Diessen, on the edge of a vast lake, the Ammersee. The trail, consistently signed with a blue crown and K symbol, wends its way through the woodlands of the Maizinger ravine before crossing open farmland to the pretty village of Aschering. Another section of tranquil forest emerges on to rolling hills and a shrine-lined path to the hill-top monastery town of Andechs.

Founded in 1455 by Benedictine monks, the monastery is renowned both for its baroque church – built after the original buildings were destroyed by fire in 1669 – and the monks' on-site brewery. The astounding rococo frescos on the church ceiling will have you craning your neck, but a tipple of the monk's potent brew

The hill-top monastery town of Andechs is famous for its beer-brewing monks

A view from Diessen, which sits on the shores of Lake Ammersee

Church tower at Andechs

will be more than enough to ease any aches en route to Herrsching, the lake port for the ferry-crossing to Diessen.

Set on the southern shore of the Ammersee, the small town of Diessen has a charming waterfront park, where old fishing nets hang from wooden boathouses and sailing boats are moored to rickety jetties. The town centre features a couple of traditional restaurants or Gasthofs, where you can indulge in delicious Bavarian fare, such as goulash soup or Wiener schnitzel. On your way out of Diessen, you can visit the city's cathedral: the Marienmuenster. The whitewashed walls sit proudly on the skyline and it is one of Bavaria's most impressive baroque buildings.

The route continues through idyllic woods and open pastures, with views to the distant Alps, and along quiet back roads to the monastery at Wessobrun, another spectacular rococo gem. You will see blue-and-white striped maypoles in many of the towns and villages along the way, and the one at Wessobrun, just outside the Gasthof zum Post, features an array of figures that reflect Bavarian rural life.

The high point of the trail is at Hohenpeissenberg, before the overnight stop at Unterbrau. The climb is not too strenuous and the astounding views, across the forested valley to the high peaks of the Alps, from the terrace of the Gasthof at the top of the ascent are worth the effort. From Unterbrau, you enter the most dramatic part of the route as you negotiate the Ammerschlucht traverse, a breath-taking path through an enchanting beech forest in a sheer-sided glacial gorge. Where necessary, wooden boardwalks span precarious drops and ladders go up rocky outcrops.

Following an overnight stay in Rottenbuch, a delightful monastery town set around a cobbled square reached via a stone gateway, the route heads towards Buching. Along the way, it passes through the

Rococo ceiling at Rottenbuch church

Wies church attracts many pilgrims

A view of the Alps en route to Buching

Overleaf: Neuschwanstein Castle sits atop a dramatic ridge overlooking Forggensee

popular village of Wies with its ornately decorated baroque church – a pilgrimage site famed for its statue of Christ, which is reported to have cried tears in 1738 – and on through serene pine forests to Steingaden. As you approach Buching, at the base of the Alps, the towers of Neuschwanstein Castle can be seen on a distant hill.

Although there are buses up to the castle, the most fitting way to arrive is via the awe-inspiring ascent through the steep and narrow

Evening light on a church at Buching

Dusk over a small lake near Füssen

Pöllat Gorge. As striking as this part of the route is, it cannot eclipse the impact of the view from the exposed, gravity-defying bridge at its top. Neuschwanstein Castle, with its fairy-tale turrets, is perched on a precipitous ridge high above Ludwig's more reserved Hohenschwangau Castle and the green plain around the Forggensee and Füssen. The king built Neuschwanstein in 1869 as a temple to Wagner's genius. Ludwig's demise may be shrouded in uncertainty, but there can be no doubts about the majesty and vision of his architectural legacy or the richness of this walk through his much loved Bavaria.

Sherpa Expeditions, based in the UK, offers tours along King Ludwig's Way. It arranges accommodation en route, daily luggage transfers, so that you only need to carry a daypack, and international flights if necessary. The nearest international airport is Munich. From there it is a 90-minute train journey to Starnberg. The walking is fairly easy for most of the route. The best time to go is between May and early October.

Ascending Pöllat Gorge

Forest trail between Wies and Steingaden

King Ludwig's Neuschwanstein Castle (left) and Hohenschwangau Castle (right) at sunset

Tiger Leaping Gorge
China

Spectacular night-time illuminations on Wanga Lou Temple, Lijiang

Widely regarded as one of China's best treks, the two- to three-day walk through Tiger Leaping Gorge offers magnificent views of the Yangtze river and the Jade Dragon Snow Mountain range.

Ascending Tiger Leaping Gorge above Walnut Garden

Chinese lanterns, Lijiang old town

The gorge is located about 70 km north of the delightful ancient city of Lijiang in China's remote Yunnan province, close to the border with Tibet and Myanmar. It is the principal capital of the Naxi tribe's autonomous county, and its old town dates back over 800 years – the old cobbled streets, lined with pagoda-roofed houses and restaurants separated by small, winding canals are captivating to explore.

Pleasant in the daytime, the city becomes particularly atmospheric at night, with a surreal mix of dimly lit shops quietly trading much as they have done for centuries butting on to the raucous karaoke scene along Xinhua Jie street, which leads off Sifang Square. Dominating the town in all directions is Lion Hill, crested with the elaborate, multi-tiered Wanga Lou Temple. At night both are illuminated to give one of the most striking city skylines you are ever likely to see.

En route to Halfway Guest House

Village in the clouds, near Daju

Clear streams tumble into the Yangtze river

Although most trekkers access Tiger Leaping Gorge from Qiaotou, an uninspiring, small market town on the main road from Lijiang to Zhongdian, it is possible to start from its other end, at Daju. Setting off from here means you avoid the gruelling ascent up the notorious 'twenty-four bends' section. It is sometimes referred to as 'twenty-eight bends', but both names fail to reflect the reality – that it is a steep, constantly weaving, energy-sapping climb.

The journey to Daju from Lijiang is in itself memorable, as you drive along a rough track through the high peaks of the Jade Dragon Snow Mountain range. Clouds swirl in and out, cloaking and revealing

Narrow canyon near Halfway Guest House. Overleaf: Rockfalls often tumble into the gorge, partly blocking the Yangtze river

the valley far below, with its small villages and the snaking Yangtze. From tiny Daju – which has no facilities – it is a short walk down the steep bank of the river to reach the ferry. Banish all thoughts of a Yangtze cruise – this mini-ferry is purely functional: slightly battered and powered by two tractor engines complete with steering wheels. When you look at the swift currents of the caffelatte-coloured Yangtze you will wonder whether the life jackets should be worn rather than kept in a plastic bag behind steel bars in the driver's cabin.

Once across the river, a winding road traverses the relatively flat valley floor before gradually ascending into the gorge, to the small

village of Walnut Garden. This is a good place for lunch with several restaurants boasting terraces that overlook the chasm. The Yangtze reaches its narrowest point here in the gorge – at the 25-metre-wide spot where, according to legend, a tiger leapt across the raging water to escape a hunter. This funnelling of the water flow creates rapids so powerful that only one of the attempts to traverse this part of the river, by a Chinese team who in 1986 rafted the entire Yangtze from source to sea, has been successful; all the others have ended in catastrophe.

Around 20 minutes from Walnut Garden the road walking ends and the high trail proper begins, just opposite Tina's Guest House. It gently climbs across open slopes with ever improving views down along the Yangtze – this section is known locally as Golden Sands river. The gorge is sandwiched between two imposing peaks, 5596-metre Jade Dragon Snow Mountain, which gives its name to the

Buddhist prayer flags flutter at a trail shrine

Several small villages are located in the gorge

entire range, and Haba Mountain, not much less a colossus at 5396 metres. The summits are often shrouded in cloud, but the sheer 2000-metre-high dark rock walls of the gorge ensure that the scenery is always spectacular.

The ascent eventually eases and the path traverses, passing a couple of waterfalls, some isolated Naxi family houses and a shrine bedecked with fluttering Buddhist prayer flags. It then reaches your overnight stop: the appropriately named Halfway Guest House, set in an enviable location in Ben di wan village. You can sip a beer or green tea on the terrace and enjoy the beckoning silence of nature, as dusk casts its subtle blue and pink light across the cliffs opposite.

High waterfalls bisect the trail en route to Halfway Guest House

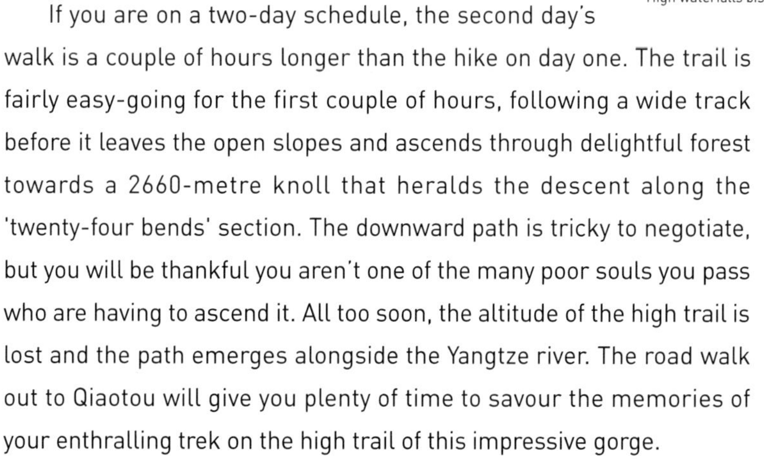

If you are on a two-day schedule, the second day's walk is a couple of hours longer than the hike on day one. The trail is fairly easy-going for the first couple of hours, following a wide track before it leaves the open slopes and ascends through delightful forest towards a 2660-metre knoll that heralds the descent along the 'twenty-four bends' section. The downward path is tricky to negotiate, but you will be thankful you aren't one of the many poor souls you pass who are having to ascend it. All too soon, the altitude of the high trail is lost and the path emerges alongside the Yangtze river. The road walk out to Qiaotou will give you plenty of time to savour the memories of your enthralling trek on the high trail of this impressive gorge.

ⓘ

The very friendly and efficient Lijiang-based tour operator In Depth China offers a range of trekking tours around Yunnan province and beyond, including guided treks through Tiger Leaping Gorge. You can fly to Lijiang from several international airports in China, such as Beijing, Kunming and Chengdu. Internal flights are relatively cheap for the distances covered and the time saved. There is a wide range of accommodation in Lijiang, including the peaceful Zen Garden Hotel, with great views of the city at night. It can get very cold at night, so take plenty of warm clothing layers. The gorge is susceptible to rockfalls and landslides, which can close off access, so take care on the trail and don't hike alone.

The Dolomites
Italy

Young, jagged and imposing, the Dolomites are perhaps the most striking mountains in Europe. Although they are a stunning location for summer hiking, they are at their most sublime in winter. Stepping into a pair of snowshoes might feel strange at first, but it will allow you to walk to parts of this snowbound wonderland that are normally reserved for mountaineers and extreme skiers.

The Dolomites range is part of the Alps and is located in the northeastern region of Italy, a couple of hours' drive north of Venice. During the First World War, the mountains were the front line between the Italian and Austro-Hungarian forces. Many remnants of their defensive systems can still be seen today, including extensive tunnels through the cliffs and the via

Summit views from 2672-metre high Sas Ciampac in Puez massif

Exploring the summit area around Sas Ciampac

ferrata (metal ladders, chains and steps) that were used to access the most difficult terrain. Today, traversing the via ferrata has become a popular mountain sport.

Although most people come here to walk during the summer months, an increasing number are discovering the attractions of snowshoeing in winter. The shoes are attached to normal hiking boots and because they significantly increase the surface area of footprints they stop walkers from sinking into the snow. Modern designs are lightweight and allow a fairly natural walking movement, so you don't need any experience to get going on them.

Two of the best centres for accessing snowshoe routes are Pedraces and Arabba. These quiet and traditional towns are set among dramatic mountain scenery in the Alta Badia region. The main

language here is Ladin, an ancient Rhaeto-Romance dialect unique to just a few areas in the Dolomites, but everybody also speaks at least Italian.

There is a wide choice of snowshoeing routes, ranging from ones that take just a few hours to overnight trips that involve a stay in a mountain hut, but it is advisable to choose a short trail for the first time out. An ideal option, a few hours long, is the Runch Hut Round, directly above Pedraces. A great feature of ski resorts is their lift systems, and on this walk you avoid the uphill graft by jumping on the Santa Croce chairlift to be whisked to 2045 metres without breaking sweat. From the lift station, the trail passes the delightful Santa Croce church and the nearby *rifugio* (mountain refuge hut) and café before gently heading up around the base of high, rugged cliffs. In deep snow, the descent back down, past isolated mountain huts, is like a fun combination of walking and skiing, with panoramic views across the valley to 2668-metre Ciampani peak and the mountains of the Puez Massif.

Some of the First World War tunnel systems have been preserved as open-air museums and one of the best is at Lagazuoi, at the start of the Col dei Bois snowshoe trail. Just below the upper cable-car station at Piccolo Lagazuoi, you can enter one of the tunnels high up in the cliff face. With regular spyholes punched through the rock, it was one of four lookout posts built by the Austro-Hungarians. The trail from here is more challenging than the Runch Hut Round, traversing steep slopes as it enters the valley below the hulking, rocky mass of Col dei Bois. On the way back, it passes through a rock tunnel before climbing through the ruins of an old military hospital.

Approaching the Col dei Bois

Rock tower at Cinque Torri

Church in Arabba

The Italians do most things in style and their mountain huts are no exception. Any thoughts of rickety, old wooden cabins and freezing in sleeping bags are banished on the epic overnight trip across the Fanes massif – an experience not to be missed. The hut at Lavarella is a chalet with hot showers, comfortable bunk beds and an on-site restaurant and bar. Thankfully, there are no lengthy climbs once you have ascended to the massif itself; just a wonderful day in an enchanting mountain wilderness, sloughing through the snow as you follow the upper reaches of the Sciarè river. On the following day, the route descends down the long, peak-lined Fanes river valley, passing through pine forests before it re-enters civilization near the tourist-honeypot town of Cortina d'Ampezzo.

If you have found your snowshoeing rhythm and your legs are feeling strong, a true big-mountain trail climbs 2672-metre high Sas Ciampac in the Puez massif. This is not for the faint hearted, as it

Late afternoon descent from Col dei Bois

Both: Dusk on the descent towards Val du Chedul

ascends some very steep terrain in a wild, remote location, but the 360-degree views of the entire Dolomites and beyond from the top of the massif are breathtaking. The descent through the dramatic Val du Chedul is also an adventurous experience.

Among the most famous rock formations in the Dolomites are the isolated limestone Five Towers (Cinque Torri) that spike the mountain skyline just a short downhill stretch from the chairlift. An easy place

Late afternoon light above Val du Chedul

Dramatic rock tunnel at Cinque Torri

to snowshoe and with hot coffee and lunch just a quick hike away, Cinque Torri is the perfect place to savour an outstanding Dolomiten winter-walking adventure.

ⓘ

Collett's Mountain Holidays offers an extensive summer and winter programme of activities in the Dolomites, including snowshoeing and skiing. It has chalet bases in both Arabba and Pedraces, and its programmes are flexible, allowing you to do as much snowshoeing as you like during your stay. The nearest international airports are either Venice Marco Polo or Venice Treviso, from where Collett's arranges transfers. You need good, sturdy walking boots to attach the snowshoes to, although they can be made to fit almost any ankle-high footwear. The snow season in the Dolomites often lasts longer than in other parts of the Alps, but late December to late April are probably the most reliable times.

Battlefields of the Somme

France

Dawn at Mill Road Cemetery

Wars are often discussed in cold statistical terms: the metres of ground gained, how many soldiers were injured or killed or the number of tanks sent to the front line. Heartbreaking as the figures from the Battle of the Somme are, walking the fields over which it was fought gives a deeper and far more moving insight into those terrible months of 1916 than the statistics can ever offer. Over 90 years on, the courage and suffering of both the fallen and the survivors still pervades the landscape.

Although the battle lasted for nearly five months, the first day still stands as one of the most deadly in the history of warfare. After it started, at around dawn on 1 July 1916, it was only a matter of hours before over 19,000 British soldiers lost their lives and 36,000 were injured. An unknown number of German troops met similar fates. By the end of the Somme campaign in November 1916 over 300,000 men on both sides had been killed and around a million more injured.

Poppies dot the landscape around Bernafay Wood Cemetery

The Thiepval Memorial to British and South African soldiers

Crops now sway in the breeze across no man's land

Simple stone crosses mark the graves of unknown soldiers at Thiepval

Located to the northeast of Amiens, around 130 km north of Paris, the Somme region today is a charming collection of traditional French villages and towns sprinkled across a mellow sea of rolling hills. The battlefields cover a small area about 25 km long by 10 km wide, so it is often possible to see, from the same location, several war cemeteries spread around the landscape. There are countless walking routes, which vary in duration from just an hour or so to a full day.

The most prominent, and perhaps the most moving, memorial in the Somme is the one at Thiepval, which can be seen from many parts of the region. A five-hour walk from Authuille takes you through the countryside around Thiepval, which saw action on the first day of the battle. Authuille cemetery itself is pleasantly located behind the village on a low valley slope. It is small in comparison with many others in the area and this lends it an extra intimacy. Throughout any Somme walk, the rows upon rows of crisply clean white headstones draw you in to their details, though many mark the graves of unknown soldiers. The dates come in clusters, reflecting the most deadly offensives, and none occurs more frequently than 1 July 1916. Whole battalions were wiped out in the blink of an eye and friends fell beside friends, as merciless machine-gun fire sliced across every inch of the open terrain and artillery rounds exploded all around.

The route continues via Blighty Valley Cemetery and Crucifix Corner to loop around Authuille Wood, which was held by the Eighth Division when the battle commenced. The German front line was just tens of metres away over a slight rise. Past Lonsdale Cemetery you see the Leipzig Redoubt. A small stand of trees and bushes atop an almost imperceptible slope, its slight elevation and the open fields all around made it a crucial German stronghold. The 17th Highland Light Infantry, from Glasgow, was tasked with attacking it on the first day and the German heavy guns mowed down the slow-moving lines of its soldiers. As you walk up the rise towards the redoubt, it is difficult to believe that anyone survived; few did. Beyond the redoubt you soon reach the memorial at Thiepval. Completed in 1932, the magnificent

French memorial in Guillemont village

Names of soldiers fill the walls at Thiepval

Delville Wood Memorial remembers the fallen South African soldiers

Pozières Cemetery

archway features the names of around 70,000 British and South African soldiers who died during the battle and whose bodies could not be found or identified.

Many memorials are worth visiting, such as at High Wood, Bernafay Wood and Pozières, but the most emotive monument is perhaps the one to South African soldiers at Delville Wood, near Longueval. Set at the end of a serene avenue of trees, it is a majestic structure with sweeping wings emanating from a central arch. In the now beautiful wood, where sunlight streams through the leaves, the trees seem to retain the spirits of all those who fought and died here.

Many troops from Commonwealth countries fought alongside the British, and one of the Somme's most impressive monuments is the

Ulster Tower remembers the 36th Ulster Division, near Thiepval

Dawn at Guillemont Road Cemetery

Newfoundland Memorial Park, near the village of Auchonvillers. It is an extensive site and a visit to it is ideal if you want a gentle walk lasting a couple of hours. The biggest attraction is the trenches that are still visible. They were miserable places, and when it rained the accumulation of water caused trench foot – a condition whereby the feet simply start to rot. As you walk through them it is easy to imagine the hopeless terror soldiers must have felt when the whistles blew for them to go over the top.

In a valley below the Newfoundland Memorial Park lies Beaumont-Hamel, set in a copse. It too saw action on the opening day of the battle, and a three-hour walk from Auchonvillers to this pretty village takes you around the most important sites. En route, you pass

Newfoundland Memorial Park

Thiepval Memorial

Morning light streams through Delville Wood

Hawthorn Ridge, scene of the first of the mighty explosions that signalled the start of the battle. At 7.20 a.m., the 40,000 pounds of explosives that the British had placed under the German lines by digging tunnels erupted into the air. At that moment, in Sunken Lane – a recessed track in no man's land – on the outskirts of Beaumont-Hamel the 1st Lancashire Fusiliers readied to attack. In the ensuing carnage, 18 officers and 465 men were killed. Walking up this simple, unremarkable lane, green with the fresh growth of spring, the powerfully moving experience of seeing the Somme at first hand is perhaps at its most poignant.

ⓘ

Walking the Somme **by Paul Reed (published by Pen & Sword Military) is a detailed and easy-to-follow guidebook to various walking trails around the battlefields. It is best to have your own vehicle to get around the region, as your choice of routes would be severely limited if you relied on the scarce public transport. Though hotels are relatively scarce around the Somme area, countless B&Bs offer a generally good level of affordable accommodation close to the main sites.**

Sunset over fields near Auchonvillers

Delville Wood Memorial

Leipzig Redoubt was a deadly German stronghold

Garden Route

South Africa

The Khoikhoi, its original inhabitants, called the Garden Route region the Land of Honey (Outeniqua). Today the area is regarded as the paradise of South Africa, a fertile and abundantly diverse landscape fringed by the Indian Ocean and lush forests, with high mountains inland. Here the scenery is ever changing and the walking is easy – perfect for a leisurely exploration of the tip of Africa.

Fransmanshoek

The Garden Route itself is a 200-km section of the N2 road that sweeps from Cape Town to Port Elizabeth, and there are many walking routes within the surrounding area, encompassing its coastal, mountain and forest terrains. With each new landscape comes a different habitat and the lure of fresh animal-spotting opportunities.

Following the striking coastline of the Indian Ocean at some stage of your journey is a must – the Knysna Lagoon and Plettenburg Bay are just two of the choice locations where you will be able to feel sea spray on your face and get close to the pounding surf with its high-rolling waves.

Boggomsbai

Sunrise, Knysna Heads

Oystercatcher Trail

Kanon Bay sand dunes

One of the latest walks to have opened is the coastal Oystercatcher Trail, linking Mossel Bay, at the start of the Garden Route, with the protected inland waters of the Gourits river. Starting from the Khoisan Cave, an ancient seashore dwelling of the now extinct hunter–gatherer clans, this four-day hike takes you through unspoilt dune systems, abundant in plant life. The Khoikhoi people used many of these plants medicinally – for example, the juice of sour figs to soothe insect bites and as an early form of lip balm. High cliffs at Pinnacle Point, and further east at Fransmanshoek, provide vantage points from which to watch the mighty ocean thunder below, while the relative calm of the broad bay at Boggomsbai attracts breeding and calving southern right whales in the winter months.

In hidden coves carved out of wind- and wave-weathered cliffs russet-coloured lichen clings to boulders, glowing a brilliant orange in the soft afternoon light. Kanon Bay, a remote beach, seems to stretch ahead endlessly, beautiful in its isolation, and backed by ever shifting

Crashing waves, Knysna Heads

windswept dunes that are reputed to be the highest in the southern Cape. Gnarled pieces of knotted wood eroded by the elements lie scattered at its edges, daily flotsam and jetsam swept in on the tide. The walk ends with a sedate boat ride across the broad reaches of the Gourits river where fish eagles can sometimes be heard, their distinctive call known as the 'voice of Africa'.

From the mouth of the river the flat coastal plateau leads to the Outeniqua Mountains, approximately 50 km away. These and the Swartberg Mountains, 100 km north of the Gourits, form two parallel ranges that dominate the southern Cape. In between lies the Little Karoo. In this semi-desert hinterland – *karoo* is a Khoikhoi word meaning dry and hard – grazing ostriches seem to outnumber people.

The 23.5-km Tierkloof Trail is ideally located in the heart of this landscape, in the Gamkaberg Nature Reserve. *Tier* or *tijger* was the name early Dutch farmers gave to leopards and, while these animals are famously rare, they have been sighted along the route.

Gouna river, Diepwalle

Sunset, Gamkaberg Nature Reserve

The Little Karoo

At the start of the walk the pink clapperbush flowers fringe the trail. The route, signed with painted leopard-paw prints, is easy to follow and leads through a deep, forested ravine before ascending to the fynbos-rich mountain plateau, a form of heathland unique to the Western Cape. All along the way there is the hum and buzz of birdsong. Dashes of flitting colour swoop past – vibrant green from a malachite sunbird or the flash of a yellow-chested bokmakierie.

The route can be undertaken as one long round trip or broken into two days if you stay at Oukraal, an overnight shelter on the plateau. From here, the undulating curves of the Swartberg and Outeniqua ranges seem to glow in the soft light of sunset. The possibility of spotting a herd of the endangered Cape mountain zebra is an added interest although these beautiful animals remain elusive.

The draw of yet another unusual species will certainly justify a visit to the richly dense woods of Diepwalle, a four-hour drive away. Just over 20 km northeast of Knysna, they are home to one of the world's few forest elephant populations. Sightings are scarce but the thought that you may come face to face with South Africa's only herd of truly wild elephants will add an extra level of excitement to your walk. Every rustle among the closely packed bushes and overhanging trees will have you stopping dead in your tracks. Three different trails allow you to explore these striking woods, which boast some of the country's largest trees, including Kind Edward's Big Tree, a 600-year-old towering giant yellow-wood.

As you hike further into the forest huge ferns wave in the breeze, their interlacing fronds sometimes almost hiding the path from view. They part to reveal the Gouna, an ambling river with brown, bubbling water that is almost the colour of cola. It is a peaceful scene – only occasionally interrupted by the distant screeches of squabbling baboons – and a perfect finale to your exploration of the tip of Africa.

Walking in areas like the Little Karoo can be unpleasant in summer, with soaring temperatures and little shade. The best times for hiking along the Garden Route are South Africa's early summer (October to December) or autumn (March to April). A hire car is recommended in order to explore the variety of walks available. If you have a limited amount of time to travel around the area, the five-day Garden Route Trail from the Wilderness National Park to Knysna Lagoon is worth considering.

The Tierkloof Trail

Kind Edward's Big Tree, a giant yellow-wood

Oukraal, overlooking the Swartberg and Outeniqua mountains

Walking the *falaise* above Ireli village

Dogon Country

Mali

Deep in the heart of West Africa, Dogon country in Mali is a remote and, to unaccustomed eyes, harsh land. To the tribes who have lived here for hundreds of years, the landscape is imbued with the spirits of their ancestors and every rock, every tree has a story to tell. A trek around the striking orange cliffs and villages of the Bandiagara escarpment – the centre of Dogon country – takes you far from the creature comforts of luxury hotels, but you will be rewarded with a rare opportunity to journey back to an ancient lifestyle at the root of human existence.

Granary houses in Tereli village

Getting to Dogon country is a journey in itself, and the ten-hour drive east from Bamako, Mali's capital, is best broken up into smaller chunks. Stopovers are possible in Ségou, Djenné – a World Heritage Site with an impressive adobe mosque – or Mopti, where you can take a relaxing boat trip along the Niger river. After the monotony of flat desert plains, the emergence of rusty orange outcrops on the approach to the town of Bandiagara will be as compelling a sight to you as it must have been to the Dogon people when they first arrived in the area, in about the fourteenth or fifteenth century.

Before heading out of Bandiagara on the main trek, it is worth exploring Songo, one of the best-preserved Dogon villages. A 15-minute drive away, it is set against a backdrop of outcrops. Every three years there is a festival here to celebrate an important rite of passage, when its teenage boys are circumcised. It is possible to ascend to the ritual cave, adorned with red, white and black figure paintings, where the boys pass three weeks in isolation; socializing, singing and playing musical instruments.

Dogon door detail, Tereli

There are several routes for trekking the escarpment, one of the most popular of which, from Sanga to Douro, takes two days with the option of an additional day walking the 18 km back to Bandiagara across the plateau. The initial drive from Bandiagara to Sanga takes around 90 minutes and follows a very rough 4WD track. For around 25 years, until 1956, French anthropologists Marcel Griaule and Germaine Dieterlen chose Sanga as the principal subject village for their intensive study of

Water well in Douro village

the Dogon people and their animist beliefs and tribal traditions. They were initiated into the tribe and their research remains seminal.

Sanga today is a sprawling collection of adobe houses, with the Dogon's trademark pointed-roof granary buildings prominent above high walls. Millet and red chillies dry on the roof tops while a constant stream of children fetch water from the village pump for the day's cooking and washing. As the trail gradually ascends further on to the plateau, Sanga slowly disappears below the horizon. On its outskirts lies a table of divination, a patchwork of symbols etched in the sand, which is used by the village *hogon* – a spiritual leader – to foretell the future.

As you cross open, rocky terrain there is little warning of what lies ahead: at the *falaise* (the edge of the plateau) the path suddenly drops down through a narrow canyon, the walls of which are lined with tombs, and emerges halfway up the cliff face above Ireli. This village boasts one of the most beautiful of the *togu na* – low, open-sided

Tombs dot the cliffs above Ireli village

Animist reliefs at the Dogu Na, Ireli

Adobe roofs of Songo village

shelters roofed with millet. These are the sole reserve of the men, who spend hours in them, resting and talking about local issues; the low roof prevents them standing up to fight if debates get heated.

From Ireli, the trail drops down to the Gondo plain and passes below the cliffs to Tereli, one of the most traditional of the area's villages and your overnight stop. The tribe's animist beliefs take their most dynamic and exhilarating form in breathtaking mask dances, and the dancers of Tereli are prime exponents of the art. The Dogon universe is based around Amma, the master who created the sun, moon and stars, and Amma's offspring the Nommo twins. These

Dancer's mask, Tereli

Spectacular mask dance in Tereli

Dogon water their cattle in the river en route to Douro

Sibi-Sibi village on Bandiagara plateau

Woman pounding millet in Songo

creator beings brought life to the planet in the form of rocks, grass, water, and every other animate and inanimate object.

Dances are normally performed at festivals and special village events, but you can also pay to see one. Drums bang and the pace is frenetic: the dancers strut and spin, and their incredible standing leaps seem to send them flying into the spirit world. The earth reverberates with the pounding of their feet and dust spirals up from the ground. The masks represent everything from *hogons* and antelope to the creation myth and even the rising and setting sun.

Before sleeping, you can gaze at a sky crammed with stars and listen to the sounds of village life drift upwards, as they have for centuries, towards the ancestors in their cliff-wall tombs: the chatter of families gathered around a fire, the rhythmic thud of pestle and mortar, and the clatter of hoofs as herds of sheep and goats are led through Tereli's narrow alleys. There are places in the world that offer far more luxury, but few are as magical as the roof of a Dogon mud hut at night.

From Tereli, the trek continues along the Gondo plain, through fields of millet, to Komokani and Nombori. The distances between

Dogon villages is generally only a few kilometres or so, but the overwhelming heat, especially after midday, makes walking more of an effort than usual. From Nombori, the trail crosses a river before making a spectacular ascent through a cliff-face canyon, where the outer wall teeters high above the plain, to Douro. After spending the night here, you can either walk back to Bandiagara or arrange to be driven part or all of the way. Whatever you decide to do, you won't forget your spiritually uplifting encounter with the beautiful people of Dogon country and their beguiling landscape.

London-based agency Tim Best Travel specializes in organizing small-group and tailor-made trips to Dogon country and other regions of Mali. It is possible to visit at any time of year. Travelling through the villages needs to be done sensitively, with respect for the people and their customs and traditions. It is essential to ask permission before taking photographs and most people expect a small payment in return; be prepared to pay without argument as this is an important source of income in the villages.

Watering spring onions on Bandiagara plateau

Child at *hogon* temple, Sanga

Fallingwater
USA

Over the last century human interaction with the natural world has all too frequently led to devastating consequences. This only serves to accentuate the pinnacle of perfection achieved by renowned American architect Frank Lloyd Wright when he integrated his architectural masterpiece, Fallingwater, into the Pennsylvania landscape. This iconic building, set among forest-clad slopes criss-crossed with a network of hiking trails, is proof that it is possible for us to live in balance with nature.

Nature and architecture mix on the cantilevered decks

Located near the town of Ohiopyle in the Laurel Highlands, part of Pennsylvania's Allegheny Mountains, Fallingwater is now owned by the Western Pennsylvania Conservancy. It was commissioned in 1934 by the Kaufmann family, who wanted a summer house at their favourite picnic spot, near a waterfall on their Bear Run property. Edgar Kaufmann Jr, had read Lloyd Wright's *An Autobiography* and been instantly won over by his holistic approach to blending architecture with nature. He told his father about him and Fallingwater resulted, reaching completion in 1939. It became famous almost immediately, when it was featured on the front cover of *Time* magazine.

Fallingwater was built across the Bear Run river waterfall

Stream, Fallingwater

Arbutus Trail in Bear Run Nature Reserve

Frank Lloyd Wright's inspiration for his organic architecture flowed from many sources, but some of his earliest influences date back to the summers he spent working on his family's farm near Spring Green in the Wisconsin river valley. He observed the subtle nuances of light throughout the day, and how the landscape changed as the sun marched across the sky; he watched the dappled rays as they filtered through the tree canopy on to the earth. Surrounded by woodland and rocky outcrops, he saw at first hand how natural structures provide enduring support for each other and form unlikely shapes and patterns. Later, Henry David Thoreau's and Ralph Waldo Emerson's writings about nature struck a chord deep inside him. All these influences came together perfectly in Fallingwater, widely acclaimed as his finest achievement.

While it is tempting to make straight for the house itself, to see it in context it is best to head first into the Bear Run Nature Reserve, just a few minutes' drive north of Ohiopyle along Highway 381. Also

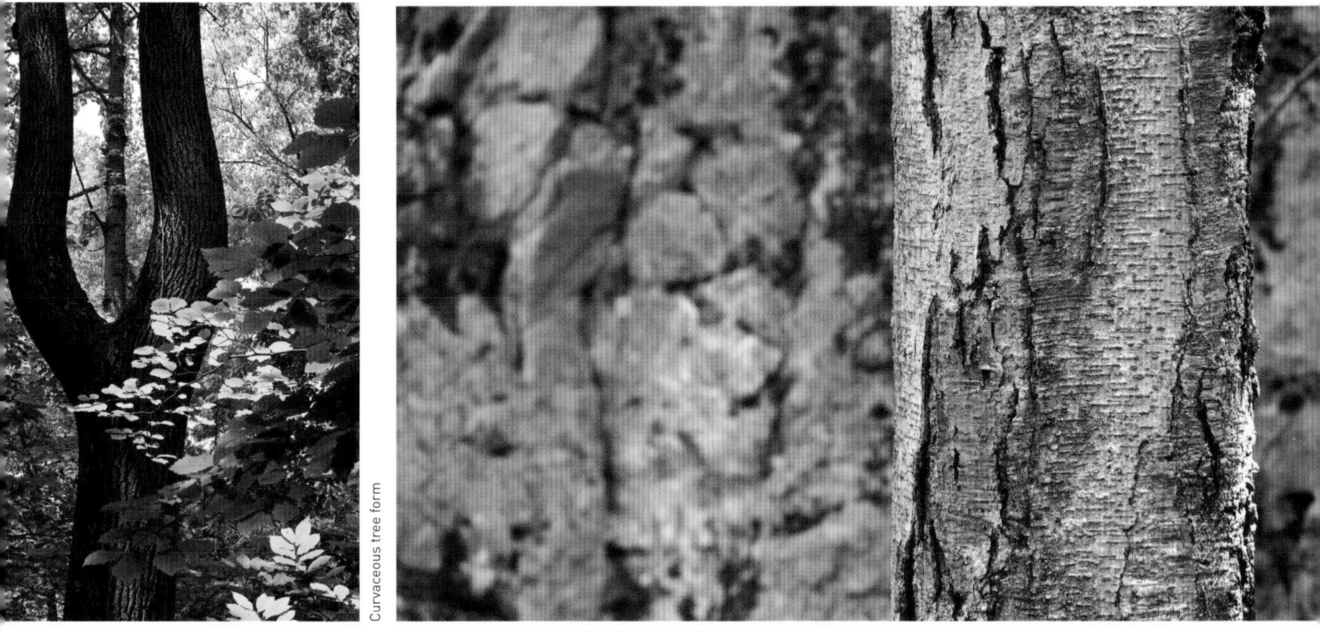

Curvaceous tree form

Tree and rock colours merge, Bear Run Nature Reserve

owned by the Western Pennsylvania Conservancy, this 2020-hectare area on the west slope of the Laurel Ridge features about 32 km of trails, which can be followed individually or linked together to form longer hikes. Whatever your choice, exploring the reserve demands a slow walking pace. The more relaxed it is, the more remarkable this undulating terrain becomes.

There are 16 marked trails ranging from the 500-metre Kinglet Trail to the 4.1-km Peninsula Trail, which takes you to a lookout high above the Youghiogheny Valley. The Arbutus Trail is recommended as

Bear Run river runs into the Youghiogheny river, seen at dusk

Stone cairn, Youghiogheny river

Bear Run stream

a gentle introduction, as it heads along relatively flat terrain through a tangle of rhododendron bushes and mountain laurel. Amble along and your eyes will steadily become attuned to the subtle beauty of the forest: the splash of sunlight on the warped trunk of a hemlock tree, the shadow of a plant falling on a sandstone boulder. The sounds of the forest begin to sink in, too: the rustle of leaves as a breeze blows through the canopy, the flutter of a bird's wing.

For a full day out you can link the Arbutus and Wintergreen trails, climb on up the wilder Bear Run Trail, and then loop around the Laurel Run Trail on to the Peninsula Trail. If you tire, there are quicker alternative routes back to the car park. To see the Youghiogheny river up close, take one of the easy trails around the Ferncliff Peninsula, near the railroad crossing in Ohiopyle, which lead to lookouts over its most impressive rapids – a worthwhile two-hour hike.

Cantilevered tree on Ferncliff Peninsula

Curved tree, Bear Run Nature Reserve

Once you have an appreciation of the surrounding landscape, your visit to Fallingwater itself will be enriched. When you walk into its grounds, past a rocky outcrop, you soon hear the waters of Bear Run stream flowing towards the property over a tumble of bedrock. When the Kaufmanns told Lloyd Wright they wanted a house that would take full advantage of a dramatic rock ledge and waterfall, they couldn't have dreamt that he would build one that spanned them. It is an astounding and daring piece of design that brings the water through the middle of the structure before it cascades below large cantilevered terraces.

The longer you spend admiring the exterior of the house, the more the subtle intertwining of nature and architecture becomes apparent. The buttress walls, constructed from sandstone quarried from the site itself, merge into the slope behind them. The terraces mirror the overhanging rock ledge below. The concrete slats of the extensive canopy over the main walkway are exquisitely shaped to bend around existing trees. Sunlight and shadow fall on surfaces with the chaotic beauty that is found in the woods of Bear Run Nature Reserve.

This meshing of nature and creative design continues inside Fallingwater. The fireplace is half cut-stone, half natural bedrock.

Main lounge, Fallingwater

Stairway leading to Bear Run stream

Canopy bends around a tree trunk

Countless framed panes of glass allow light to flood in through the windows, which reflect the surrounding trees and landscape in such a way that it is, at times, impossible to tell what is interior and what is exterior.

There are several trails around the property, the most striking of which leads to a lookout downstream where the valley widens. From here, the house is dwarfed by towering trees and rising slopes, and the multi-tiered drop of the waterfall is as mesmerizing as the house itself. Here it is the wonder of nature, not architecture, that is overwhelming – just as Frank Lloyd Wright intended.

ⓘ

Access to the interior of the house is strictly controlled by the Western Pennsylvania Conservancy, with limited numbers of visitors allowed in each day, except on Mondays when the house interior is closed. Tickets are usually booked up well in advance, but it is possible to get on to an interior tour on the day if the allocation is not already taken up. The tours range from 55 minutes to two hours in duration. The grounds are open daily and less restricted, and you can buy entry tickets on arrival. No tickets are necessary for the Bear Run Nature Reserve. Trail maps are available in the car park.

Sculpture on cantilevered deck

Interior and exterior become one at Fallingwater

Cantilevered decks span the river

Darjeeling Tea Trek

India

Dawn over Kangchenjunga

As dawn slowly creeps across the Himalayas, an awesome amphitheatre of the world's highest peaks, rising above terraced tea plantations, comes to life. The snow-encrusted faces of Kangchenjunga, Lhotse, Makalu and Everest, the greatest of them all, are brushed by the delicate pink glow of the morning light. If you are not a serious mountaineer, this trek through the foothills of the Indian Himalayas is one of the best ways to experience these formidable summits.

It all begins in Darjeeling, a hill station in the northern ramparts of West Bengal, northeast India. Spread around a crescent-shaped ridge, it is seated beneath the mighty bulk of Kangchenjunga, which, at 8598 metres, rises majestically centre stage. Beneath the mountain,

deeply forested slopes and terraced tea gardens drape downwards.

After an early morning drive from Darjeeling the trek begins in Maneybhanjang, a small bazaar of spilling stalls. From here the trail climbs sharply through thick woodland. In the surrounding glacier-gouged valleys, clouds sweep in and all that can be heard in the billowing mist is the rumble of 4WD vehicles on the nearby track.

It is a landscape that has a spiritual resonance for many of its inhabitants, none more so than those at Chitrey Monastery. Here the sound of chanting Buddhist monks, their heads diligently bowed as they recite the holy scriptures in a shadowy corner of the prayer room, can be mesmerizing. Outside, a line of chortens, monuments to the dead, stand sentry.

Chortens at Meghma Monastery

At Lamedhura, 6.5 km from the start of the trek, the daily ritual of tea-drinking begins. As you sip your steaming infusion, chickens peck at your feet and cows wander freely. After passing a scattering of small-holdings at Meghma the path meanders upwards to the campsite at Tumling. From the centre of the village, mighty Kangchenjunga, the world's third-highest peak, rears over the nearby hills. At sunset, clouds can hover at its base with the sky glowing a resplendent pink.

This is one of two places on the route – the other is later at Sandakphu – where the sunrise makes staggering out of bed worth while. Here dawn transforms slowly into day as the surrounding mountains of the Kangchenjunga range are illuminated. The view is awe-inspiring and these peaks will remain visible for most of the day.

When the time comes for morning tea you will be handing your passport in to border control officials at Gairibas in order to re-enter India. Quite unknowingly, you will have have briefly walked into Nepal. The route weaves an intricate line between the two countries, which

Sunset on the Singalia Ridge

Sunrise at Sandakphu

means that at times you can literally have one foot in India and the other in Nepal. By afternoon tea you will be overlooking the lake at Kal Phokari, your overnight stop.

The next morning the path winds down to the Valley of Poison (Bikhebhangang), so named for its abundance of poisonous plants. The next 4 km is a steady walk upwards to the village of Sandakphu.

At 3636 metres, Sandakphu is the high point of the route and potentially offers the grandest panorama of the entire trail. Commanding spectacular views of mountain slopes covered with rhododendrons and silver firs, this is the one point on the route where you may be lucky enough to see all the big summits. Watching the sunrise from a rocky outcrop vantage point on the edge of the village you not only see the entire Kangchenjunga range stir slowly to life as the first light hits its bulky mass, but on clear days Everest will also be part of this awesome all-surrounding mountain vista. The classic peaks rise loftily skywards and prayer flags flutter around you in the breeze.

Lamedhura teahouse

Prayer flags and Kangchenjunga

Porter's basket, Jubari

Glenburn Tea Estate

It is hard to drag yourself away from such a view but there is more walking to be done. From Sandakphu there are a number of options, depending on how much time you have available. For a four-day trek you can head south and straight down to finish in Rimbick. But if you have five days, heading west takes you along the high ground of the Singalia Ridge and one the most rewarding parts of the trek.

This is where you will feel that you are in the heart of the Himalayas, with mountain peaks all around you and tree-covered slopes sweeping gracefully downwards. Further on, there is an almost Alpine feel to the route as you walk through rolling green pastures – until, that is, you come across the occasional grazing yak.

You could continue along the ridge to Phalut, where you would overnight and then return to Rimbick via an additional stopover at Raman, a six-day trip. Alternatively you can take five days by choosing the path down from Sabargram, through rain-carved stream beds and bamboo forest. This allows you to overnight at the pretty village of Sri Khola, alongside a tumbling, boulder-choked river.

Sri Khola to Rimbick is an easy 7-km walk through lush bush with the Raman river twisting below like ropework. Along here signs of

Mani prayer wall, Tumling

everyday life return, with people from the surrounding hill villages using the path to go about their daily business. Women carry on their backs woven baskets piled high with grass, men herd donkey trains loaded with goods and children in uniforms hurry to school.

There is possibly no more fitting an end to the trek than to have afternoon tea – and no better place to drink it than on a working plantation. An hour's drive from Darjeeling is the Glenburn Tea Estate, where the beautifully preserved colonial-style Burra Bungalow has been home to generations of tea planters since the plantation was established in 1860. As the monsoon-plucked Darjeeling leaves infuse in the teapot, a speckled patchwork of vibrant green tea bushes tumbles below.

Carefully consider the weather when planning a visit to Darjeeling. The best months for trekking are April and May when the magnolias and rhododendrons are in bloom or October and November when visibility is at its best. Tim Best Travel organizes bespoke itineraries that include transport, fully staffed treks with porters, guides and a cook, and end with a stay at the Glenburn Tea Estate. Jet Airways has daily services from Delhi and Kolkata to Bagdogra, Darjeeling's nearest local airport. The town is a further four-hour transfer by taxi or bus.

Darjeeling dawn

Meteora
Greece

Great Meteoron Monastery

Agios Antonios Monastery

At Meteora, in central Greece, grand rock spires crowned with Byzantine monasteries glide skywards above the sweeping Thessaly plain. Amidst these lofty pinnacles, a place of spiritual retreat for monks of the Greek Orthodox church, smaller spiralling outcrops resembling whipped cream are topped with overhanging scrub. In between, a network of paths connects these religious sanctuaries, enabling walkers to make their own spiritual ascent.

Roussanou Monastery is surrouned by Meteora's towering pinnacles

The area first became the focus of religious attention in the eleventh century, when devout hermits seeking solitude built rudimentary wooden structures that clung to the rock faces. More ascetics followed them and made use of existing caves gouged in the weathered rocks.

The first monastery was founded in the fourteenth century by the monk Athanasios, on a rock he called Great Meteoron (Megalo Meteoron) – which later gave its name to the whole complex of monasteries: Meteora. The word means 'suspended in the air', and is

an apt description for these precariously sited buildings, whose wooden galleries and corniced roof tops crown the formidable rock towers that rise from the vast Thessaly flatland. In their heyday there were 24 working monasteries with ornate frescos and vast libraries containing rare handwritten manuscripts.

The target of German mortars during the Second World War and used by communists during the Greek civil war (1944–9) the mona-

Dawn over the Thessaly plains

Dramatic cliffs at Kalambaka

steries sustained heavy damage. But a period of revival followed and in 1988 Meteora was named a UNESCO World Heritage Site.

The mighty sandstone rocks on which the monasteries were built stand like sentries, weathered by the ravages of wind and rain. Given their scale as they rear up from the plains, it is almost impossible to believe that this area was once under water. It was a huge lake that eventually drained into the Aegean Sea, and a mass of stones, sand and mud that had previously formed a single cone was split by erosion. Seismic vibrations, strong winds and heavy rain further sculpted the twisting rock formations of today's Meteora.

With a busy road now connecting the six inhabited monasteries, which are open to visitors, and the bustling town of Kalambaka spread beneath the rocks, it may be difficult to comprehend that Meteora was once a spiritual outpost, reached only by the truly determined.

Wind and rain sculpted the rock spires of Meteora

However, the well-worn twisting paths that led the monks to their sanctuaries still lace through the pinnacles, gradually weaving upwards. As they have done for centuries, they continue to take travellers into the heart of this majestic geological garden.

The village of Kastraki, 2 km north of Kalambaka, nestles beneath a weighty outcrop, on which the uninhabited Holy Spirit Monastery (Agio Pneuma) stands, and is the starting point for a

Evening light on Roussanou Monastery

Stone carving, Great Meteoron Monastery

number of routes. A couple of cafés edge the central square where morning customers sit in the sun, sipping ice-cold frappés charged with strong Greek espresso coffee.

One of the most popular paths, a leisurely day-walk of approximately 10 km, heads north to the secluded church of Agios Georgios Mandelas where paved steps lead up from the road into beautiful woodland. Normally a peaceful section of the route, on St George's Day, 23 April, it is transformed as villagers line the path eagerly awaiting the young men of Kastraki, who climb the soaring rock wall above the wood to place cloths in a small cavern shrine. The fluttering scraps of fabric look almost like prayer flags.

The route winds through the woodland down to the main road and crosses it a few hundred metres from the monastery of Agios Nikolaos, set on an isolated column close to the tooth-like Doupiani rock. An initially cobbled pathway leads gently upwards through a steep-sided gorge where moss-laden branches almost obscure the track in places. It then passes the Varlaam and Great Meteoron monasteries, where stone stairways lead to bulky wooden doorways that provide a glimpse into a remote devotional way of life.

The trail continues roughly northwards and takes you through secluded woods past cairns that mark the way to the uninhabited Ipapanti Monastery. The austere Vlahava monument, an incongruous metal statue of a lone swordsman, overlooks rolling farmland below. Now a dirt track, the path winds back through this gentle countryside giving further views of Meteora. Here tall, yellow grasses frame the west-facing rocks and in the late afternoon, as the sun begins to dip, the scene is bathed in a golden glow. The route then leads southwards to the bulky mass of Doupiani and the road back to Kastraki.

The imposing nature of Meteora's jagged columns often makes the monasteries above them seem inaccessible – and for the most

Church window, Great Meteoron Monastery

Roussanou Monastery

Holy Trinity Monastery

The uninhabited Ipapanti Monastery clings precariously to the cliff face

Rock pinnacles at dawn

Roussanou Monastery is home to a community of nuns

Great Meteoron was Meteora's first monastery

A sunset walk above Kalambaka

part the rock faces themselves can only be explored by equipped climbers using ropes. But it is possible to walk to the Holy Spirit Monastery above Kastraki, a round trip of about two hours. A path round the base of the pinnacle on which it is built continues past the wooden-slatted platform of a cave hermitage, known as the monastic prison, and takes you into a narrow inner gorge. Halfway along this a pathway leads up to the monastery, a cave shrine gouged into the rock wall.

A scramble on to the rocks above the shrine will reward you with views across the Thessaly plain to the encircling Pindos and Antichasia mountain massifs and the Peneios river below; for a moment you may well feel that you are suspended in the air.

ⓘ

The monasteries of Meteora can be busy, particularly during the summer months when it is worth while arriving early to avoid the crowds. The best walking temperatures are in spring and autumn. The nearest airport is at Thessaloniki, about a four-hour drive away on good roads. It is also possible to take a train from Thessaloniki or Athens with a switch at Larissa. If you travel from Athens, take a morning train so that you can enjoy the spectacular scenery as you pass through the mountains between Livadia and Lamia.

Canals of Amsterdam
The Netherlands

One of Amsterdam's 'Seven Bridges'

The hubbub of café life spills a chorus of chattering voices beside them, clock towers peal their chimes above them, while bicycle wheels clink and rattle on the cobblestone bridges that cross them. Wandering along the waterways of Amsterdam is the perfect way to soak up the laid-back charm of a city carved by its canals.

The major ones are collectively known as the *grachtengordel* (girdle of canals) and ring the city centre. On the adjacent cobbled walkways, in a harmonious jumble of offices, houses, restaurants and bars, you will find the life and soul of Amsterdam – at work, rest and play.

Canal boats and townhouses both offer city centre living

The Amstel river, one of Amsterdam's busiest waterways

This radial network of waterways – a total of 165 wind neatly through the city – plots an intuitive pathway, so route-finding is easy: you simply choose a canal and follow it. Very quickly it will lead you to another and then another. While it might be tempting to join the 600,000 bikers speeding through the streets, or hop aboard one of the many boats that cruise the canals, this is a city perfectly suited for wandering, strolling and ambling. You never have to go far to find the next interesting stop-off.

From the Singel, Amsterdam's original medieval moat, three other canals, built during the Golden Era of the seventeenth century

as part of the city's urban-regeneration scheme, spread concentrically outwards: Herengracht, named after the *heren* ('gentlemen' or, sometimes, 'lords') who were responsible for its construction; Keizersgracht, which commemorated Maximilian I – the Kaiser and Holy Roman Emperor – and Prinsengracht, named after Prince William of Orange. This area, where the rich once lived, is now the ideal starting point for walks. Interconnecting streets and canals offer further opportunities for exploring.

Gable-gazing is a must on canal streets lined with slender five-storey buildings. The most famous is the seventeenth-century

Anne Frank's House is a popluar attraction

Gable-topped townhouses line the city streets

residence at 263 Prinsengracht, where teenage diarist Anne Frank and her family hid for two years during the Second World War. Despite the house attracting almost a million visitors annually, it isn't difficult to get away from the crowds on Prinsengracht. As you walk along the canal you can soak up the atmosphere at some of the city's unique brown cafés. These hark back to the time when Amsterdam was the richest port in the world, with a steady stream of incoming traffic, people and goods. They offered up *gezelligheid*, a kind of Dutch cosiness or conviviality that was sorely missed by sailors on long sea journeys. Dotted throughout the city, they have barely changed, with their dark wood-panelled interiors, smoke-stained walls and often sand-covered floors.

At Bloemstraat, just off Prinsengracht's main thoroughfare, is Café Chris. A tap house since 1624, it is opposite the Western Church (Westerkerk) and is where its thirsty builders went to receive their wages. Heading north along the canal to Egelantiersgracht reveals Café 't Smalle. Beyond the pretty canalside patio with its line of fluttering sunshades, creaking wooden doors lead inside to reveal a moment caught in time. Orderly glass bottles line the shelves,

Leliegracht and Keizersgracht are lit at night

Moored houseboats on the *grachtengordel*

wooden seating carves shadows in the dim light and travellers wander in to pull up a stool at the panelled bar and catch up on news.

Much of the charm of Amsterdam is in what remains behind closed doors. The hidden courtyards and secret gardens of the *hofjes* (almshouses) are another telling find. Often the only clue to

Early morning on the Keizergracht, one of the main canals

their existence is a small nameplate hinting at the oasis that lies behind it. Some of the gardens are open to the public, and at 107 Egelantiersgracht a green door leads through a narrow, blue-tiled corridor to an inner courtyard. Here, among swaying foxgloves, the sounds of the city fade away.

Short cuts and stop-offs are all part of experiencing Amsterdam on foot, and almost every corner on Prinsengracht beckons you to a detour. If you dip into the Nine Streets (Negen Straatjes), where each boutique-filled lane looks like the next one, you will find almost anything you may want to buy. One store, the White Teeth Shop (De Witte TandenWinkel), is dedicated solely to toothbrushes and dental care.

Kloveniersburgwal, the outermost of the three eastern canals in the medieval part of Amsterdam

Modern buildings line the Ijhaven waterfront

Bridge leading to Scheepstimmermanstraat

The far eastern end of Prinsengracht leads to the wide reaches of the Amstel river and the seventeenth-century sluice gates that allow the city's canals to be flushed with fresh water. Just above these is one of Amsterdam's most famous sights: the Skinny Bridge (Magere Brug), a hand-operated wooden drawbridge.

In a city that can boast 1281 different bridges it's easy to find yourself lingering simply to take in how much they are a part of Amsterdam life. Boats glide gracefully beneath them and people lean on black metal railings or thick stone edges to catch a moment's sun, while the shrill peal of a bicycle bell warns walkers to move to the side. A deviation worth making is to Herengracht Bridge, from where the graceful stone arches of the famous seven canal bridges can be spied. At night they light up in a kaleidoscope of converging colours.

Every aspect of life can be seen around Amsterdam's canals and now, as the city expands, these waterways continue to define its urban spaces. In the waterfront area bordering the IJ, the waterway artery that allows access to the city, there are new developments and exciting architecture. On Java island you can find a modern twist of geometric lines and bolder vivid colours redefining the traditional canal house. And if you cross to Borneo island from Sporenburg, via either of two distinctive curving red bridges, you can wander along Scheepstimmermanstraat with its eccentric façades.

In the midst of this maze of modern glass-fronted buildings the brick Lloyd Hotel is an intriguing testament to change. This former youth prison, which still retains a host of original features including bars on some of the windows, has been carefully redesigned and now provides accommodation, a bar and restaurant. In front a broad walkway overlooks the water's edge and, as the sun dips over the water, Amsterdammers can be spotted taking their final canalside walk for the day.

Amsterdam is a year-round destination, but the summer months attract the biggest crowds to main attractions like Anne Frank's House. The city offers accommodation of all ranges and to meet all budgets. Well worth it for its sweeping panoramic views is the Amsterdam Movenpick, which sits between the old town and the newer waterfront developments on the IJ. The main canal areas are all within walking distance.

The Nemo Science Centre, Oosterdok

Inca Trail
Peru

Soaring and plunging among the ice-clad summits and deep green valleys of the Andes, the Inca Trail is probably the most famous walking route in the world. Following part of a vast network of paths, this epic four-day trek links a series of ruined settlements, many of which offer a far more evocative experience than Machu Picchu, the trail's illustrious and much visited endpoint.

Cusichaca Valley from Llulluchapampa

At its height, between 1438 and 1533, the Inca Empire stretched from central Chile up through the Andes mountains to southern Colombia. To control this vast and often inhospitable region, the Incas constructed almost 23,000 km of mainly stone-paved trails. Relays of runners used these to bring news to all parts of the empire; and goods, borne by llamas, could be rapidly transported. Like modern-day porters, these runners could negotiate the steep and at times treacherous steps of the paths at bewildering speed, and it is reliably thought that they could make the 1980-km journey from Cuzco, the Inca capital in modern-day Peru, to Quito, Ecuador, in just five days. The trails also helped the army to move quickly between trouble spots.

Cloud Town (Phuyupatamarca) is one of the most inspiring campsites

Final steps towards Dead Woman's Pass, above Llulluchapampa campsite

Cuzco is still the main centre of the Peruvian highlands, and any excursion on the Inca Trail starts here, with a train or bus journey to one of several trailheads. The most popular, commonly known as km 82, is reached by bus. However, if you take the Machu Picchu train to km 88 – a three-hour journey from Cuzco – you will not only have a far less crowded trek, but also experience one of the most spectacular rail journeys in the world. The track switchbacks dramatically up the brown earth flanks of the Cuzco Valley before skirting the edge of the Urubamba river in the shadow of immense Andean peaks.

Ruins at Willkarakay

Porters at the Llulluchapampa campsite

From the train stop at km 88, an old cable bridge takes you over the raging brown waters of the Urubamba to arrive immediately at the Q'ente campsite. An overnight stay here will give you the chance to take a three-hour round-trip hike to the rarely visited ruins of Machu Q'ente and Huayna Q'ente, set high on the precipitous slopes of Cuzco Valley. Early next morning, a cup of tea served in your tent heralds the start of the trek to Machu Picchu. After following the banks of the river through eucalyptus forests, the trail turns into the Cusichaca Valley, past the vast stone terraces of the Patallaqta ruins.

Wiñay Waina ruins

Cloud forest trail near Cloud Town (Phuyupatamarca)

Nearby, a worthwhile hour-long detour takes you up a steep path to the ruins of Willkarakay, spectacularly located high above the valley on an exposed ridge.

Back on the main trail, a relatively gentle walk alongside the Cusichaca river, through a narrow valley dotted with small settlements, leads to Huayllabamba, a popular campsite for hikers starting from km 82. It is also the last resting place before the incessant climb towards the trek's highest point: the 4215-metre Dead Woman's Pass (Paso Warmiwañusca). As you pass along uneven stone steps through luxuriant cloud forest, the gradient is at times severe with the path arrowing upwards. The mountain tops above you swirl in and out of cloud, and the temperature starts to fall; snow is not unusual on these high sections of the trail. After camping overnight at Llulluchapampa, it is just an hour or so to the pass where, weather permitting, there are wonderful views across layers of jagged mountains, beyond which lies the Amazon rainforest.

As steeply as the trail climbed to the pass, it now plunges into a deep valley, to another campsite at Pacamayo, before immediately

Campsite above Cloud Town (Phuyupatamarca)

climbing again past the circular stone ruins of Runkurakay, a *tambo* (staging post) for the Inca runners. The path steepens further to the top of a second pass before threading through a rock tunnel and descending past Chaquacha Lake to the Sayacmarca ruins, set on a promontory overlooking the Aobamba Valley. With the Amazon not far away, the temperature and humidity are both significantly higher here. The trail eases as it traverses, often on high ramparts with sweeping vistas, towards Cloud Town (Phuyupatamarca).

Camping on the dramatic ridgeline above the ruins of Cloud Town is a highlight of the trek, especially if the weather conditions are good: the 360-degree view swings from the Urubamba river and the peaks around Machu Picchu, past cloud forest to the magnificent white giant that is 6271-metre Salcantay, Peru's second most prominent peak after Huascarán. Even after nine knee-jarring hours on the trail from Llulluchapampa this glorious scene, bathed in gentle evening light, is one to send your spirits soaring.

The final section of the trail takes around five to six hours and is primarily one long descent down unfeasibly narrow and steep steps

Storm clouds over Cusichaca Valley

to the exquisite ruins at Wiñay Waina. A winding traverse through moss-draped forest then leads to the Sun Gate (Intipunku), the entry point to Machu Picchu. The wildness and intimacy of the Inca Trail is suddenly lost among the crowds of day visitors at this iconic lost city, which was voted one of the New Seven Wonders of the World. While it is an impressive sight, set atop a mountain ridge above the Urubamba river, and was undoubtedly a major goal at the outset of your trek, it is likely that you have already enjoyed the most treasured moments of your world-class walk.

Abercrombie & Kent offers both a standard and a deluxe version of the Inca Trail. On the latter you are accompanied by a masseur who will ease your weary legs, have daily camp showers and eat extraordinary food conjured up on the mountain by experienced chefs. It is no longer possible to hike the trail independently: you have to go with an accredited tour company and use porters and a guide. A couple of nights in Cuzco, at 3600 metres, before starting the trek, and walking slowly, will help you to acclimatize to the height of the passes. The guides used by Abercrombie & Kent are trained in mountain first aid and carry oxygen in case of problems.

Previous pages: Machu Picchu, the Lost City of the Incas

Runkurakay was a staging post for Inca messengers

Snow-capped Salcantay, from Cloud Town (Phuyupatamarca) campsite

Exploring the beautifully preserved Machu Picchu

Wolong Nature Reserve
China

Pandas thrive at Wolong breeding centre

River overview en route to Wuyipeng

The mist-clad, deep gorges and high mountains of Sichuan province in southern China are home to about 85 per cent of the planet's remaining wild giant pandas. While it is possible to trek through much of the area in the hope of seeing these rare and instantly adorable animals, the attraction of the Wolong Nature Reserve is that you are guaranteed a close-up encounter with them at its world-renowned breeding centre.

Wolong is about 140 km northwest of Chengdu, the provincial capital. Before heading out from the city, it is worth exploring the various

Young panda cub in Wolong Nature Reserve

Buddhist temples and getting your first fix of these black-and-white bundles of fur at the impressive panda-breeding centre on its outskirts – reached via the aptly named Panda Road. Rather than the cramped zoo conditions you may be expecting, the giant pandas, along with some very rare arboreal red pandas, are housed in lush, spacious, cage-free pens that have been designed to reflect their natural habitat. An extensive network of paths winds its way around the centre, and you can easily spend half a day here watching the older pandas feast on bamboo shoots and the youngsters frolicking in the trees. The arboreal

red pandas are far smaller than their giant namesakes, resembling racoons. A visit to the centre is a wonderful experience but don't, as many tourists do, consider it a replacement for travelling to the far wilder and more atmospheric Wolong Nature Reserve.

The journey there takes four to five hours, and it is likely that the haphazard standards of Chinese driving will have you slightly frazzled by the time you arrive in the astounding Pitiao Valley. The valley is so narrow and the mountains so high and steep that it is almost impossible to see the tops of the surrounding peaks from inside the vehicle. In contrast to the natural beauty all around, Wolong town itself is strangely dour, a simple strip of jumbled shops and restaurants strung out along the valley floor. Many visitors merely pass through for the day, but such haste is not advisable as it takes time to fully appreciate the pandas and explore their habitat. The Wolong Nature Reserve covers around 200,000 hectares and in addition to the giant and arboreal red pandas is home to a number of other rare animals, including the elusive snow leopard.

Monk in Chengdu

The panda-breeding centre is about 5 km back down the valley from the town, and it is worth making the effort to get there early in the morning when the pandas are more active. Set into the lower slopes of the mountains, it adjoins the Pitiao river and features huge natural pen areas that stretch down its banks and up the valley flanks. The centre is hugely successful in breeding pandas, with around 60 or so currently in residence. While you may take sufficient pleasure from simply visiting it, there is an extensive volunteering programme through which you can assist the full-time staff for as many days or weeks as you wish. This way you get to be up close and personal with the giant pandas, and gain access to areas that are normally closed to visitors.

Monastery in Chengdu city centre

Dramatic suspension bridges cross the gorge in Hero Valley

Wooden waterwheel in Hero Valley

Cloud over the peaks of Pitiao Valley

River trail off Pitiao Valley

Various short trails lead up the slopes to the higher pens, where you can appreciate the pandas' agility as they clamber up the tall trees to rest. Without a doubt, the star attraction is the gang of young juveniles, who play for hours on end, chasing, tumbling, and climbing – and occasionally falling from – the trees. You will probably find that one visit to the centre is not enough to fully enjoy their antics.

Once you have had your fill of panda fun at the breeding centre, there are numerous options for exploring the more remote parts of the Wolong Nature Reserve and getting to see the habitat of the wild pandas. Treks range from half a day to a couple of weeks if you are particularly hardy and committed to spotting a wild panda. A riveting one-day hike takes you up into Hero Valley, which joins the Pitiao Valley on the road towards Dengsheng.

After passing an old waterwheel the trail soon begins its relentless ascent, at times up relatively steep steps, into a sky-scraping narrow gorge. Rock tunnels allow passage through some of the more difficult terrain, and the gorge is crossed on awe-inspiring

rope bridges. If you take the longest trail, which is highly recommended though a little treacherous in places, you plunge back down to the banks of the tumultuous river on several occasions. The trail was built to allow researchers studying giant pandas access to the area, and what it lacks in terms of maintenance it makes up for with thrilling views and a *Jurassic Park* atmosphere.

After two to three hours you reach the researchers' camp at Wuyipeng. The old buildings are a little dilapidated, but a brand-new visitor centre with accommodation is being built. Vast enclosures, covering many kilometres, have been erected on this part of the mountain and there is the opportunity to track down some of the semi-wild pandas that have been released here. The search goes off established trails and can take anything from 20 minutes to a few hours, depending on where the animals are. The thrill of glimpsing them for the first time eclipses all previous panda encounters back at the breeding centre. With care and silence, it is possible to approach them and watch for 10 or 15 minutes as they munch away contentedly on bamboo shoots, or maybe carrots brought as a treat by the tracking guides. Being so close to a panda in its natural habitat inspires a deep hope that these wonderful animals survive and thrive.

Arboreal red panda, Chengdu

ⓘ

At the time of writing (2008), the road from Chengdu to Wolong was undergoing major reconstruction and was closed for much of the day, so the journey time for the 140-km trip may be longer than the usual four to five hours. Permits are needed to hike into Hero Valley. These can be arranged through the panda-breeding centre at Wolong or via a number of agencies that offer panda-tracking tours. There are currently only two hotels in Wolong, so booking ahead is almost essential; the Wolong Hotel is the more comfortable option. There is significant development in the town in anticipation of increased tourism once the road work is completed. There are many trails in the Wolong Nature Reserve and guides from the breeding centre may be willing to lead you on some of them – it is not advisable to attempt to walk them independently as they are not waymarked.

Ennerdale Water, the most westerly lake in the Lake District National Park

Coast to Coast
England

Two coasts, three national parks and the chance to cross an entire country are just some of the features that make the Coast to Coast walk an enduring classic. This 307-km route links the Irish Sea and North Sea, and is a testament to the dedication and passion of perhaps Britain's most famous walker: Alfred Wainwright.

The climb up from Ullswater leads to Angle Tarn

Best known for his pictorial guides to the Lake District, Wainwright expanded his vision beyond the boundaries of the Cumbrian fells he loved so much. In 1973 *A Coast to Coast Walk*, his illustrated guidebook to the long-distance trail he created through the valleys, hills and moors of northern England, was published. The route is not, however, a nationally recognized footpath and does not carry any official status. It offers one way to cross the country – through the Lake District, Yorkshire Dales and North York Moors national parks – but there are many potential variants. It was this sense of possibility and the joy of route-finding that Wainwright championed so enthusiastically. He encouraged hikers to adopt their own approach and seek out alternatives to his suggestions.

As a result there is no fixed direction in which to tackle it. Wainwright's preferred route begins in the west at St Bees and takes you eastward to Robin Hood's Bay, just south of Whitby. This has become a popular choice for hikers, as the push of the prevailing winds is behind them. But many choose to start in the east and keep the Lake District as the dramatic climax to their walk. Whatever your choice, Wainwright conceived the Coast to Coast so that it can either be broken down into smaller sections that are completed individually over a period of time, or – as many favour – so that it can be done as one continuous walk over a two-week period.

Thousands of people embark on the route each year, the lure of the opposing coast spurring them onwards. If you start in the west,

The Lakeland frontier is reached at Ennerdale Bridge

Wainwright advises that you dip a booted toe in the Irish Sea at St Bees and a naked foot in the waters of Robin Hood's Bay. There will be times when this refreshing meeting with the North Sea can't come soon enough.

The walk gets under way by traversing the high cliffs of St Bees Head, where nodding rosebay willowherb sways in the wind and seagulls squawk and dive-bomb. It then meanders across easy countryside, passing Cleator Moor, leading ultimately to Ennerdale Bridge. Here, at the head of Ennerdale Water, you truly get the sense of being on a frontier, as the distinctive shapes of the Lakeland fells that Wainwright loved so dearly, and which he described as 'paradise on Earth', rear ahead.

Journey's end at Robin Hood's Bay

Farms near Reeth village, Yorkshire Dales National Park

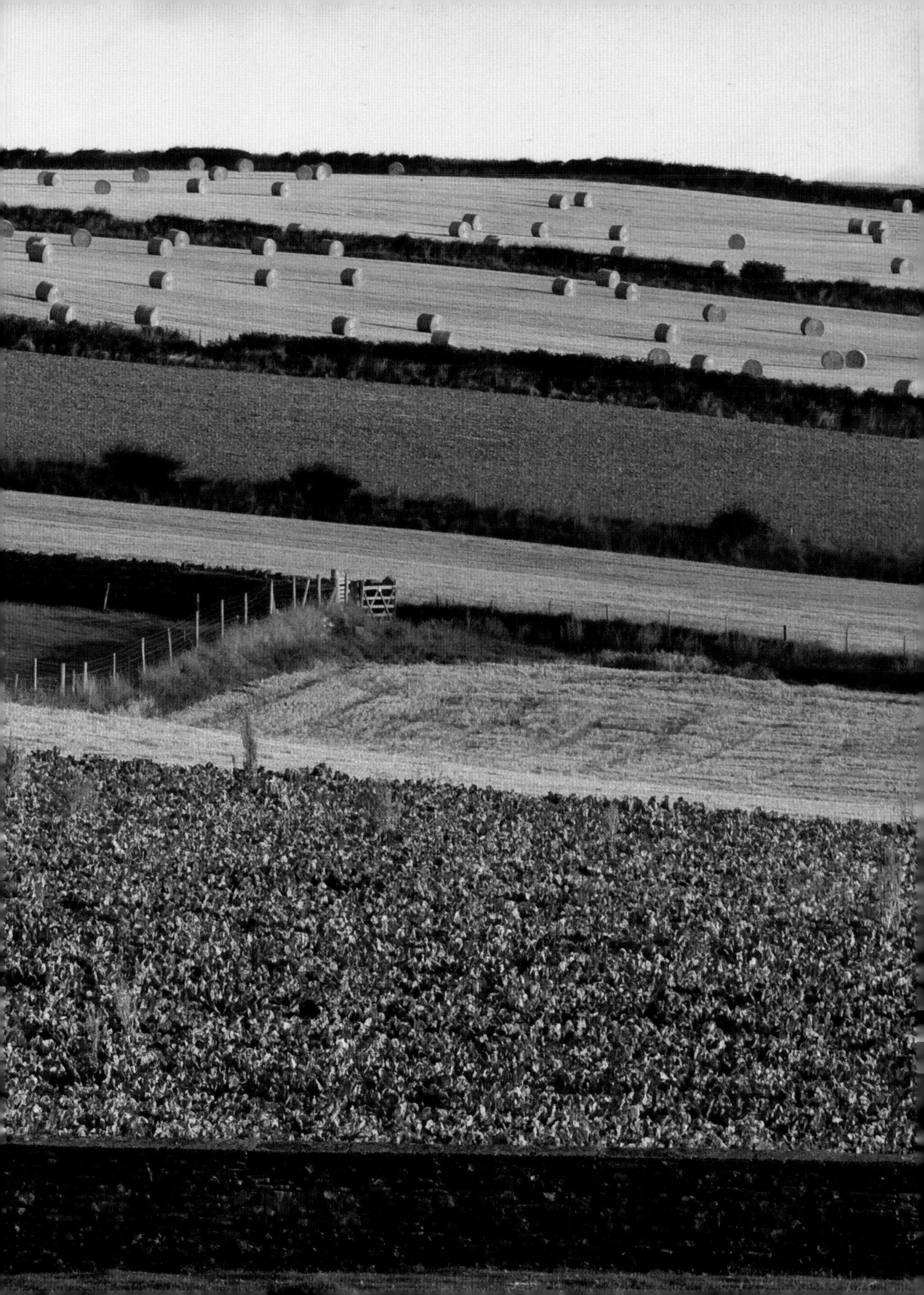

Grosmont, a 1950s station on the North York Moors Railway

Previous pages: Fields overlooking St Bees Head

Twisting street in Robin Hood's Bay

If you don't have time to undertake the whole walk, and only want to select a single section, it would be hard to find a rival to the one that takes you through the Lake District. Spanning three to four days, it marches across the heart of this famous national park, often along passes and packhorse routes carved by quarrymen many years ago. In doing so it takes in such well-known highlights as Helm Crag, rising loftily above Grasmere, home to William Wordsworth, as well as a multitude of tumbling becks, isolated tarns and lakes such as Ullswater and Brothers Water.

A highlight of the route comes as you climb out of Patterdale and on to the Straits of Riggindale, a narrow pass that leads down from the summit of High Street and follows the Roman road that once linked Ambleside and Brougham. Just above this narrow spine the path eases upwards to Kidsty Pike, which, at 780 metres, is the highest point in the walk. Beneath its distinctive rocky pinnacle, Haweswater reservoir shimmers and far beyond, on a clear day, the softening slopes of the western Pennines beckon.

What lies between the Lakes and the Pennines is different again. After passing the ruins of Shap Abbey you reach the pretty market town of Kirby Stephen and then the distinctive Nine Standards – a collection of cairns used as county-boundary markers. Ahead, sheep farms and a patchwork of drystone walls and lush green rolling fields herald your entrance to the Yorkshire Dales.

Swaledale awaits, with its meandering river, tumbling waterfalls like Wain Wath Force and the sleepy settlement of Keld, an isolated outpost of farms that is the halfway point of the Coast to Coast walk. A path along the river and onwards to Reeth takes you through some of the prettiest landscapes in the Dales. Alternatively, Wainwright's traditional path follows higher ground through the intriguing ruins of Swaledale's lead industry.

Then follows the market town of Richmond, the most fortified and perhaps the most elegant settlement on the walk. It has many well-preserved Georgian houses as well as a Norman castle, dating from the eleventh century, that perches impressively on a rocky outcrop above the Swale river.

Climbing towards Kidsty Pike above Brothers Water

Hasty Bank, North York Moors National Park

Dusk at Ennerdale Bridge

The route continues eastwards through rich, flat farmlands – the heart of the Vale of Mowbray – and onwards to the Cleveland escarpment, which gives entrance into the North York Moors National Park. Here the landscape glows purple when the heather is in bloom.

The final stretch will have you hankering for a glimpse of that long-awaited sea. Impressive cliffs lead to shapely Robin Hood's Bay where a dinky town of narrow, twisting streets clusters at the bottom of a steep rise. There is only one thing left to do once you get there: it is time, as Wainwright instructed, to unlace your boots and dip your toes in the waters of the North Sea.

ⓘ

This walk can be undertaken at any time of the year although the spring months, when there are fewer people, are preferable; booking your accommodation in advance is always advisable. Various companies offer bag-transfer services, which will help to lighten the load, as you will only need to carry a daypack.

Early morning stroll on St Bees Head beach

Sunset views towards the Irish Sea from above Cleator Moor

One of the planet's iconic features, Mount Kilimanjaro rises above the Tanzanian plains like an ice-crested stairway to the gods. It is the tallest free-standing mountain in the world and the highest peak on the African continent, and every year thousands of people are drawn to its slopes in the hope of standing atop its snow-clad summit.

Acclimatization hike from Barranco Hut

At 5895 metres above sea level, this solitary, inactive volcano is not in the Earth's upper league of lofty mountains, but with the plains that surround it languishing around 4600 metres below its summit, the first glimpse of it as you fly into Kilimanjaro airport, near the town of Moshi, is both daunting and breathtaking. It was first climbed in 1889 by a local guide, Yohanas Kinyala Lauwo, along with a German climber, Hans Meyer. But it wasn't until 1936, when Ernest Hemingway published his short story 'The Snows of Kilimanjaro' in *Esquire* magazine, that the mountain began to enter the wider public consciousness. Since then the numbers of people attempting the climb have increased dramatically, so you will not find yourself trekking alone.

Mount Kilimanjaro

Tanzania

Kilimanjaro peeks through afternoon cloud above Barranco Hut campsite

The giant endemic lobelia (Lobelia deckenii)

First views of Kilimanjaro on the Umbwe route

There are several recognized routes to choose from, the most popular of which is the Marangu, where you stay in basic mountain huts during the five- to six-day trek. The six- to seven-day Machame trail, via the Shira Plateau and Lava Tower, is the current favourite for those looking to avoid the Marangu crowds. However, the preferred choice of many of the local guides is the Umbwe route, which also takes six to seven days. Tagged as the most difficult of the climbs, the

Umbwe is also one of the most beautiful. For the first two days, before it merges with the Machame and Shira trails at the Barranco Hut campsite, it is far less trodden than the other main paths.

One of the most striking features of trekking up Mount Kilimanjaro is experiencing five distinct climatic zones, from the semi-arid lower slopes, through montane forest, moorland and highland desert to the arctic conditions around the summit. As you set out on the Umbwe route you are immediately encircled by lush forest, where colobus monkeys swing through the canopy. Occasionally,

Ascending through cloud forest on the Umbwe route

local villagers scuttle past you on the trail carrying plants and tree leaves used for everything from cooking to bedding.

On the first day, the six-hour trek starts gently before the trail steepens towards the overnight camp, set in a small clearing among a twist of trees at just below 3500 metres. Although altitude can suppress appetite, a substantial evening meal supplies essential energy for the next day's climb – the section that has earned the

Spectacular view of Mount Meru from the top of Barranco Wall

Umbwe its tag of being the most difficult route on Mount Kilimanjaro. Relentlessly steep, it takes around six or seven hours, but the upside is that you should be distracted from the effort by the stunning scenery en route.

The path climbs through a fairytale land of juniper trees dripping with wispy, pale mosses, which filter the sunlight into an ethereal glow. The ridgeline grows ever narrower until it seems you are almost walking in the air, with plunging, forest-clad valleys on both sides. Now and then, clearings give stunning views across the plains far below to the soaring bulk of 4566-metre Mount Meru, Kilimanjaro's only mountain neighbour, far off to the west. Eventually, the shining white glaciers on the summit of Kilimanjaro appear high above you. It is inspiring to see them, but they still seem distant even after the day's long climb, and this will bring home the challenge involved in getting to the top of Africa's highest peak.

After the 3900-metre-high Barranco Hut campsite, spectacularly set below the southwest flank of the mountain, the route gains

Cliffs above the Western Breach

relatively little altitude over the next couple of days. The Umbwe used to follow a more direct line up the Western Breach, but this was closed in 2006 after a serious rockfall that claimed the lives of three American trekkers. It now traverses from Barranco Hut to the Barafu Hut campsite, at 4600 metres on the southeast flank.

The imposing Barranco Wall is ascended on a precipitous path, and the trail then eases around the mountain before a sharp descent and subsequent ascent herald your arrival at Barafu Hut – the base camp for the summit attempt. This often starts at midnight, so nervousness increases as darkness descends and you wait for the late evening wake-up call. At this altitude it is very cold, no matter what the time of year and, when the sky is clear and the stars are twinkling in their millions, the temperature is likely to be well below freezing. Every available layer of clothing is needed for this part of the trek.

This last day is by far the most epic. It takes eight to ten hours through the night to climb the 1400 metres to the summit at Uhuru Peak, with its vast volcanic craters and harsh, black rock terrain.

Sunset on Kilimanjaro at Barranco Hut

Dawn above cloud-covered Moshi

Following your triumphant arrival there, and a brief appreciation of the breathtaking views over the plains below, there is a steep, three- to four-hour descent back to Barafu Hut for a snack break. The next four or seven hours are spent descending to one of the lower campsites on the Mweka route or all the way to the park gate. The steep and oversized steps pound your knees, but the sense of achievement at standing atop the roof of Africa makes such momentary suffering worth while.

ⓘ

Innovative tour operator High & Wild, based in the United Kingdom, offers guided trips on the Umbwe route. These include rest days, which significantly increases their success rate in getting clients to the summit. It is also pioneering the use of the latest Himalayan mountaineering-style oxygen systems, where oxygen fed through the nose is used for the final ascent. It is imperative to investigate your trek operator, to ensure they are not taking logistical short cuts, which can affect your chances of reaching the summit and may threaten your health, or offering low prices through not paying their porters properly. Five-day treks, offered by several companies, are often too short to allow most people to acclimatize properly. Many people suffer with some degree of altitude-related sickness. Acute Mountain Sickness is a very serious condition and can be fatal, so read up about the symptoms before going.

Dusk view of Mount Meru from Barafu Hut

Amphitheatre at Phaselis

Winding below the Toros Mountains and along the Mediterranean coastline of southwest Turkey, the Lycian Way transports you through the enchanting landscapes of classical history. The Greeks, Persians, Romans and Ottomans all made their mark on the Lycia region, and Alexander the Great marched through it on his way east. The modern-day path takes you along old trading routes to remote beaches and ruined ancient cities.

Strung out along the fringe of the Teke Peninsula, the 500-km trail runs from south of the tourist hot-spot city of Antalya in the east to

Ruined outpost at Olympos

The Lycian Way
Turkey

terminate south of Fetihye, on the west side of the peninsula. Although southwest Turkey, and especially Antalya, is renowned as a resort-holiday mecca, the Lycian Way is refreshingly distant from the nightclub scene, both in kilometres and atmosphere, and takes you into remote areas. Despite the wildness of the region, many parts of the walk are moderately easygoing, as the route meanders over coastal headlands, through juniper and cedar forests, and along tranquil beaches.

The Lycian Way was the inspiration of Kate Clow, a British expatriate who saw the potential in creating Turkey's first long-distance

Beach leading to Phaselis

Trail above the Mediterranean Sea

Forest trail to Phaselis

footpath by linking established walking trails, mule paths, forest tracks and quiet backcountry roads. As with all such paths, it is possible to pick shorter sections to walk, to suit the time you have available. An excellent week-long hike is from the mountain village of Ovacik – on the eastern side near Gedelme, not the village of the same name at the western end of the route near Fetihye – to the lighthouse at Kilidonya.

About four hours after leaving Ovacik the trail descends into the steep and deep Kemer Gorge, where clouds cling to the rock walls and the river flows rapidly below a Roman bridge. An overnight stop at nearby Camyuva village allows for a relatively leisurely start to the next day's walk, to the ruined Graeco-Roman city of Phaselis. The trail initially climbs on to a ridge line from where an old aqueduct carried water to the city. Ahead, the imposing snow-crested bulk of 2388-metre Mount Olympos, a fairly constant companion during the hike, dominates the skyline.

The first glimpses of the blue waters of the Mediterranean are

Dusk over bay at Phaselis

mesmerizing as you descend a long valley towards the Inceburun headland, and skirt high above a series of bays. A beautiful forest walk, where half-overgrown marble tombs emerge from the undergrowth, leads to Phaselis. With three harbours, the city was an important and wealthy trading centre and fell under the control of, among others, the Greeks, Alexander the Great, the Romans and, in its latter days, pirates.

Set among the woodland that edges the turquoise sea, the city boasts elegant, tall stone arches – the remains of the aqueduct – that lead on to its wide, colonnaded main street. Halfway along this, set on a small hill, is the old amphitheatre with wonderful views to distant mountains. At the southern end of the street you pass through Hadrian's Gate to a sweeping bay, before rounding a headland and following a long beach to reach Sundance Ranch – a peaceful place to stay.

The route now becomes wilder, ascending and descending a succession of headlands with panoramic vistas over the Mediterranean. After traversing the isolated beaches at Chrome and Maden, the trail

Çirali beach

climbs again before dropping swiftly down to Çirali – about a seven-hour walk from Sundance Ranch. Set back from an almost endless and relatively deserted beach, this charming village is a succession of small pensions, some set among lemon groves, and is an ideal place for a rest day.

A short taxi ride and subsequent hike into the hills behind the northern end of Çirali leads to the eternal flames of the Chimaera. Thought to be a mixture of natural gases, including methane, which

Bay at Olympos

Skywater river at Olympos

ignites on contact with air, they leap out from vents in the rocks. Local mythology has it that the flames come from a mythical fire-breathing creature, the Chimaera, which resembles a cross between a lion, goat and snake.

Near Çirali, at the southern end of the beach, is the enthralling ruined city of Olympos. Situated at the mouth of a beautiful gorge, along the tree-lined Skywater river (Göksu river) that once had shipping

Approach to Çirali beach

Shepherd's hut

access to the sea, it is a wonder to explore. Overgrown and little excavated, it is strewn with sarcophagi, tumbledown buildings and temples. If you ever longed to be a pioneering archaeologist, half a day wandering its streets and paths will come a close second best. Olympos was once part of the Lycian League, a small group of powerful cities that held sway over the entire region before it fell under the influence of Cilician pirates.

Past Olympos, the Lycian Way heads inland and climbs into mountains where strawberry trees with silky smooth, red trunks form part of an enchanting woodland straight out of a fairy tale. It is a long, remote trek on rough trails to Adrasan, some 16 km away, with no villages en route to disturb this inspiring encounter with nature. In spring and summer, wildflowers fill the glades, birds flit among the trees and tortoises rustle in the undergrowth.

The final day, from Adrasan to Kilidonya lighthouse, is another lengthy trek – about 22 km – though the terrain gets a little easier.

The path gradually climbs into hills, passing a deserted camel farm, before it returns to the coast and passes through forest high above the sea and numerous isolated bays. The lighthouse is an old but still functioning gas-powered beacon on the edge of Cape Kilidonya. At sunset, as you watch it rhythmically flash its warning along this magnificent coastline, you can savour your time on one of the world's great but lesser-known long-distance trails.

ⓘ

On Foot Holidays, based in the UK, offers a range of self-guided and guided walking holidays across Europe, including the Lycian Way. They arrange transport from Antalya, the nearest international airport, overnight accommodation and luggage transfers, allowing you to carry just a small daypack during the walk. The best months to tackle the Lycian Way are April, May, September and October. It is too cold in winter and far too hot in the peak summer months. The route takes you through some remote areas and you should be prepared for bad weather, although it is more likely to be pleasant and sunny.

Kilidonya lighthouse

Karst Country
Slovenia

Predjama Castle

Set in a notch at the northeastern border of Italy, and relatively little known, Slovenia is fast becoming Europe's hottest new hiking destination. Although most walkers head for its Alps, the adjoining Karst country offers perhaps the most enthralling mix of landscape, culture and history. With Slovenian wine, delicious home-grown food, vast cave systems and a chance to see the famous Lipizzaner horses, walking the Karst is a revitalizing step into a bygone age.

After a chequered history as part of Yugoslavia, Slovenia finally gained its independence in 1991. Although the break-up of the Yugoslavian bloc had started after Tito's death in 1980, Slovenia was

Vineyards cover the Karst hillsides

the first country to secede, sparking a ten-day war with the then Serb-led Yugoslav government. It has successfully shifted to a market economy and secured full membership of the European Union – no mean feat in such a short time.

Although there are many possible walking routes across the Karst plateau – the name comes from the Slovenian *grast* and means limestone landscapes weathered and dissolved by water – an excellent itinerary for a week of walking takes you from Predjama Castle to the astonishing cave system at Skocjan.

Predjama Castle is reached on a five-hour loop walk from Hudicevec, where you stay on a farm and have your first chance to taste

Farmhouse at Hudicevec

teran, a spicy red Slovenian wine. The track threads its way among rolling hills until it drops into the Lovka Valley, where the castle is dramatically set in a cavern at the base of a 123-metre cliff. It was first established in about the twelfth century, but what you see today was primarily built by the Kobencl family during the sixteenth-century Renaissance period. From its top floor you can enter the large cave behind it. Another cave system below the castle, part of which you can explore on a guided tour, runs for more than 13 km to the Vipava Valley. The walk back to Hudicevec is a gentle woodland stroll via the rural villages of Smihel and Strane. Life here seems to have stood still for centuries and a horse and cart is still a popular mode of transport.

From Hudicevec, the route heads northwest along quiet country roads through Lozice and Podnanos, before becoming a trail again at Podraga village. Vineyards cover almost every slope, and the path winds through the terraces. Slovenian wine is not well known, but it is exceptionally good and the local people may well invite you to join them in sampling their latest vintage.

After climbing again to Goce, the trail descends through Slap and turns west towards Gaberge. It takes you along a low ridge with expansive views across distant hills before ascending to an overnight stop in the charming village of Stanjel. Set on a prominent hill top, with the tower of St Daniel's Church its most obvious landmark, this medieval village was first settled by the Halstatt people during the late Bronze to early Iron Age period. Allow plenty of time to explore its narrow, cobbled streets, old stone houses, castle remains and the grandiose Ferrari Garden, which boasts the most inspiring views of the entire walk – across the Vipava Valley back to Mount Nanos.

After leaving Stanjel, you meander southwards across typical Karst terrain of woodland sprinkled with limestone boulders and rocks. Sinkholes are a peculiar feature of the landscape. Many of

Pumpkins at Goce farmhouse

Farm pond reflects Mount Nanos, Hudicevec

Church doors, Slap

Teran vineyard in the Brda

these large, saucer shaped depressions in the plateau are used for growing crops and grazing animals, as they offer natural protection from the *burja* – the powerful wind that gusts across the region during winter. There are numerous examples on the trail towards Tomaj from Brje; they are sometimes unused and shrouded with trees, so be careful if you wander off the main path.

A real culinary treat awaits you at the Skerlj farm stay in the village of Tomaj, which is enveloped by acres of *teran* grape vineyards. Its owners conjure up delicious dishes featuring home-produced *prsut* (thin slivers of air-dried ham, known as prosciutto in neighbouring Italy), wine from their own vineyard, freshly baked bread and tasty vegetables plucked straight from their garden.

Overindulgence at dinner will serve you well on the five-hour walk

Lipizzaner dressage show, Lipica

from Tomaj to Lipica, via the large town of Sezana. The botanical garden here is a delightful spot for a break, before you start the long haul down an arrow-straight forestry track and through idyllic Karst woodland to Lipica. The town is famed for its horse stable, which is the home of the Lipizzaner breed. These magnificent, strong stallions are capable of the most demanding dressage routines and are exported to the renowned Spanish Riding School in Vienna, Austria. A tour of the stable is well worth while, but don't miss the daily dressage show, where you see the horses in breathtaking action.

The final day is a shorter walk, just three and half hours along forest tracks and through the town of Lokev to what for many people will be the highlight of the week: the fantastical Skocjan caves. Almost 6 km in length, they boast what is thought to be the world's

Lipizzaner horse performing

largest-known underground canyon, a 100-metre-deep, 3.5-km-long gorge carved by the rumbling waters of the Reka river. As you edge through the subtly lit cave on a dramatic rock path halfway up the wall, the most awe-inspiring moment is crossing the Cerkvenik Bridge, which spans the canyon and is 45 metres above the river. It is an epic finale to a memorable walk through one of Europe's least-known treasures.

Dawn from Stanjel

Skocjan caves

ⓘ

On Foot Holidays, based in the UK, offers a range of self-guided and guided walking holidays around Europe, including walks around the Karst country of Slovenia. It will arrange for airport transfers, accommodation at the various farm stays and move your luggage each day. The region is best accessed from the international airports at Trieste, in Italy, or Ljubljana, the Slovenian capital. Throughout the Karst, the walking is generally easy to moderately difficult, with no big mountains to conquer. The trail through the Skocjan canyon can be slippery and the height may affect vertigo sufferers.

Awe-inspiring canyon above Reka river within Skocjan caves

Great Ocean Walk

Australia

The Twelve Apostles at sunset

Few countries, if any, can match Australia when it comes to magnificent wild beaches and awe-inspiring coastlines. Sandwiched between the Otway Ranges and the often tempestuous waters of Bass Strait and the Southern Ocean, the 91-km Great Ocean Walk on the coast of Victoria takes you on an invigorating journey through tangled forests to remote bays and deserted beaches. Along the way you will be reminded of the early days of European settlement, and encounter koalas and kangaroos. The finale is the extraordinary Twelve Apostles – towering sea stacks sculpted by the pounding surf.

Waves crash ashore at Castle Cove

Inaugurated in 2006, this long-distance route takes eight or nine days to complete and runs from Apollo Bay, a two-and-a-half hour drive southwest of Melbourne, to near Glenample Homestead. The rather inexplicable and inglorious official end point – the homestead is no longer open to the public so the route terminates in an isolated car park – means that most people continue to the Twelve Apostles, a kilometre further on, and Loch Ard Gorge, about another hour away, for a more fitting climax to their walk.

Shortly after leaving Apollo Bay, the route skirts around the Marengo Reefs Marine Sanctuary, and takes you past Storm Point and on to Shelly Beach. Although the Great Ocean Walk primarily follows the coastline, there are several sections that detour inland, and the climb from Shelly Beach to Elliot Ridge and back down to Blanket Bay is the longest at around three hours. The trail passes through a beautiful twist of coastal shrub entangled with ancient myrtle beeches before following Parker Road, an old 4WD track amid

Parker Road forest trail

Koala and joey

giant ferns, mountain ash and soaring gum trees. Black wallabies – also known as swamp wallabies – can sometimes be seen bounding through the bush, as you begin the descent back to Blanket Bay, the end point for day one.

An inspiring place to spend a night or two is the Great Ocean Ecolodge, a 20-minute drive from the bay – the hosts pick you up and take you back to the trail. Owned and run by dynamic young ecologists Shayne Neal and Lizzie Corke, it is an environment research centre and refuge for injured wildlife. With acres of eucalyptus forest in its grounds, it is ideal for spotting koalas, and at dawn and dusk you can sit in the lodge and watch kangaroos and wallabies foraging near by.

Back on the trail, the 3.5-km section to Parker Estuary skirts high above the sea through more enchanting forest, before descending quickly back to the shoreline. After crossing the Parker river, the

Cape Otway lighthouse

low-tide route has you scrambling over rocks and boulders, and along pristine beaches, before climbing to reach Cape Otway lighthouse. The combination of stormy seas and rugged coastline was disastrous for many ships during the early years of Australia's exploration by Europeans. Rounding the cape to reach Melbourne was notoriously difficult and the lighthouse, the first in Victoria, was built in 1848 in an attempt to reduce the number of shipwrecks. The prominent white tower has become an iconic image of both the state and the Great Ocean Road – the motoring equivalent to the walk. A telegraph station was also built on the site in 1859, allowing direct communication between the mainland and Tasmania. The lighthouse beam was eventually extinguished in 1994, but it is still possible to climb the 18-metre tower for spectacular views over Bass Strait to the left and the Southern Ocean to the right.

Kangaroos at Great Ocean Ecolodge

The highlight of the following day's hike to Castle Cove is walking along lengthy Station Beach, which is pounded by a relentless march of swells and waves. At its southeastern end is Rainbow Falls, a tumble of fresh water over colourful mosses. Walking through sand is slow going, but it allows you more time to be awed by the power of the ocean, as it

Anchor of the *Marie Gabrielle*, Wreck Beach

Surf at Station Beach. Overleaf: Twelve Apostles at dusk

crashes on the shore just metres away. After crossing a bridge over the Aire river the trail narrows, and rises and falls over a series of small headlands below striking orange cliffs to delightful Castle Cove. Another excellent place to overnight, in nearby bed and breakfast accommodation, the cove can be magical at both dawn and dusk.

The walk continues on to Johanna Beach. Wild, remote and at the mercy of the ocean's wrath, it is one of the highlights of the route and wandering along it for an hour or two, watching the full fury of Mother Nature, is a revitalizing experience. After traversing Milanesia Beach and ascending steeply to Moonlight Head, the trail heads inland again before emerging on the coast at the Gables lookout.

The next day, you encounter some remarkable reminders of the fates met by many sailors and passengers who ventured to these parts during the nineteenth century. At the suitably named Wreck Beach, there are anchors from the *Marie Gabrielle*, which floundered in 1869, and the *Fiji*, which hit the rocks in 1891. From the beach, the trail follows a sandy 4WD track to Princetown before entering Port

Walking along Johanna Beach

Sunrise at Castle Cove

Castle Cove

Campbell National Park. Winding through dunes, it ends near the unmarked track to Glenample Homestead. It is a short road walk on to Gibson Steps and the Twelve Apostles. Four of the sea stacks have collapsed, the latest one in 2005, but the eight that remain are still breathtaking, especially around sunset and sunrise when the light fires up their orange cliffs. You can easily spend a couple of hours exploring here before heading on to Loch Ard Gorge along quiet backcountry tracks.

The gorge is a series of inlets with impressive sea stacks, caves, islands and coves. It is named after the *Loch Ard*, which ran aground here in 1878, and you can enjoy your final lunch on this magnificent walk near the cave where the only two survivors, Tom Pearce and Eva Carmichael, huddled together awaiting rescue.

Johanna Beach

Loch Ard Gorge

Victoria-based walking-holiday operator Auswalk offers a range of supported tours for the Great Ocean Walk, either self-guided or guided. Covering the entire trail or shorter sections, they organize your pick-up and drop-off each day, overnight stays and daily luggage transfers. Carrying just a daypack is a major advantage on sandy beaches and the longer climbs. The trail is well set up, with numerous access points that give options on how much of it to walk, and campsites for those who want to carry their own gear. It is essential to know the times of the high and low tides – tables are available in local stores. There are points on the walk where the tide dictates your route; the low-tide routes, when safe, are often the best. There are poisonous snakes along the trail, so be aware of them and read up on how to deal with any encounter and the necessary first aid if bitten – a thankfully rare event.

Takesi Trail

Bolivia

Lake Titicaca is the world's highest navigable lake

Morning light on the Royal Mountain range (Cordillera Real)

Dramatic, brooding and laced with history, Bolivia is a living, breathing landscape of legend. Here you can literally step through time and walk to the origins of the Inca dynasty on Sun Island (Isla del Sol), and follow the Takesi Trail, an ancient, paved trading route that stretches 43 km from the high Andes to the gateway of the Amazon.

While Bolivia offers an abundance of walking opportunities you won't be going anywhere immediately if you fly directly into La Paz. Located at 4058 metres, it is the world's highest capital city. At such a height the rarefied air may well make your head spin, so it is essential to allow yourself time to acclimatize before you embark on the higher ground of the Takesi Trail. Part of this process will allow you to explore the extraordinary Inca culture and its remarkable history.

Less than a two-hour drive from the city, the huge expanse of Lake Titicaca, the highest navigable lake in the world, is an ideal place to

En route to Chincana ruins, Lake Titicaca

adjust to conditions with some easy walking trails. Equal in size to Corsica, its striking blue waters lick at the edge of the windswept Altiplano. An almost entirely straight road runs out of La Paz. It is speckled with smallholdings and simple low-slung brick houses and flanked by the awesome jutting bulk of the Cordillera Real range.

Lake Titicaca is actually two lakes joined by the Straits of Tiquina. To the north, in the larger lake, Lago Mayor (or Chucuito, which means

Rock sculptures, Sun Island

Terraces, San Baya Peninsula

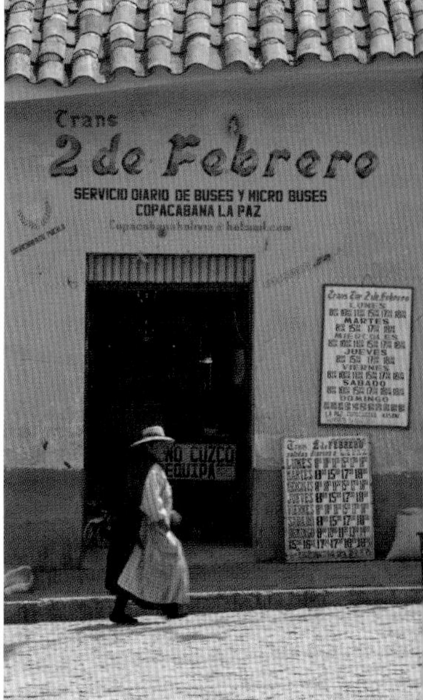

Copacabana, a pilgrim town on the shores of Lake Titicaca

'fertility'), are Sun Island and Moon Island (Isla de la Luna), key locations in the Inca creation myth.

Sun Island is widely regarded as the place where it all began, the cradle of the formidable Inca nation, or *tiksi marka* (the place of origin). While there are a number of creation myths, the most popular suggests that Viracocha, the creator god, took a handful of land and a handful of water from the lake and created his children, Manco Kapac

Traditional Aymara life continues on Sun Island

Llamas are used as pack animals

and Mama Ocllo, who were charged with the task of finding somewhere to base Viracocha's people. They left the high plateau and discovered Cuzco – in Peru – the eventual capital of the Incas. At the northwest end of the island is a sacred rock, called the Puma Stone – 'Titi Kaka' in the Andean Aymara language – which is worshipped as the birthplace of the Incas and gave the lake its name.

The site became the ultimate destination for pilgrims, who forged a trail across the spine of Sun Island. Starting on the eastern edge from Pilcocaina, the once resplendent sun gate, it took them to the Puma Stone and the Chincana Temple, the ruins of which are believed to predate the Incas and extend back to the Tiwanaku (AD 600–1100). This sophisticated civilization was noted for remarkable developments in agriculture, including advanced irrigation systems.

Allow a full day for the Sun Island trail, which will take you vividly back through history. At Chincana, a sacrificial stone, where virgins were killed and offered to the gods, remains a brutal testament to the demands the Inca deities made on their worshippers. The route ends at the Sacred Fountain (Fuente Sagrada): traditionally pilgrims drank its waters to prevent them abusing the fundamental cosmic laws by lying, being lazy or stealing. Also known as the font of eternal youth, it is rumoured to knock ten years off your age, and drinking from it may well be the final, enlivening part of your acclimatization process.

The ancient trading routes of the Tiwanaku and the Incas are defining features of the landscape and have become popular with walkers. Four different Inca trails surround La Paz and link the majestic high Andes with the Yungas, a subtropical region where citrus trees, coffee and coca grow. The three-day Takesi Trail is perhaps the easiest of these.

The journey to the trailhead, roughly two hours by minibus, takes you along a twisting road below the strange, fluted formations of the

Reed boat, Lake Titicaca

Urus-Iruitos, a floating reed island village

Chojlla River, Takesi Trail

Valley of the Souls (Valle de las Ánimas), which widens to reveal awesome views of Illimani, the 6439-metre mountain that dominates the La Paz skyline. Snow-capped peaks tumble on either side, tumultuous clouds build overhead and below you llamas roam freely in tranquil, dusty fields.

The trail begins by steadily climbing a broad valley past Mina San Francisco, a former silver mine, to the Takesi Pass (Apacheta) at 4630 metres. This three-hour section takes you across some of the best examples of traditional Inca paving stones. As you gradually climb to the top of the pass it is common to find that the clouds you may have seen earlier are lingering. At a cairn amidst the swirling mist it is traditional to make an offering to Pachamama, the Inca earth mother and a goddess of fertility, by adding a stone and throwing a few drops of alcohol on the ground.

The uphill work is over and most of the walk is now downwards, snaking through the high mountains and past the waters of Lake Wara Warani. More Inca paving stones line a route to the tiny hamlet

Aymara woman and llama, Lake Titicaca

of Takesi, a remote outpost that once served as the main stopping point for traders passing through. Nowadays most travellers camp a little further down, next to the tumbling waters of the Takesi river.

The next section takes you from the rugged mountains of the high Andes into cloud forest, where temperatures soar and bamboo plants grow alongside rose bushes. Jukumarini (rare Andean bears) still roam wild through this thick vegetation.

The thin line of the trail flashes white against this veil of green, clinging to the steep-sided valley as it curls down to the village of Kakapi; seemingly precariously placed, the buildings look ready to slide down the slopes at almost any moment. Here a lush, trellised garden provides a potential camp-site where hanging vines and sweeping clouds add to a distinctly jungle feel.

After Kakapi, the final day's walk brings you to the tumbling Chojlla river, a boulder garden of fast-flowing white water, which signals that you are nearing the end of the trail. There is one last climb up to the village of Chojlla, after which your final challenge is surviving the rough jungle road, with its cascading hairpin bends, that takes you back to La Paz.

Illimani summit can be seen from La Paz

ⓘ

The Bolivian trekking season is generally regarded as running from May to September, with the most stable weather from June to September. If you fly directly into La Paz, a period of acclimatization is essential before you attempt any form of trekking. London-based travel specialist Tim Best Travel provides full advice and organizes bespoke tours throughout Bolivia, including fully staffed treks on the Takesi Trail with English-speaking guides.

Entering Cardiac Canyon

The Wave, North Buttes

Not even Salvador Dali with his creative genius could have conjured up the surreal landscapes to be found around Coyote Buttes. Multilayered rock formations in countless shades of pink, purple, orange and yellow have been sculpted into unimaginable whorls by wind, rain and flash floods. One of the most extraordinary places on the planet, hiking through it is at times like making your way through a fanciful geological cake mix.

Coyote Buttes
Arizona, USA

Coyote Buttes lies in northern Arizona, near the Utah border, and is most easily accessed from Page, a small town set above the dramatic Glen Canyon dam. Surrounded by major national parks, such as Bryce Canyon to the north and the Grand Canyon to the south, Coyote Buttes and its environs are often bypassed, so exploring the canyons and outcrops there rarely involves dodging crowds. Just one word of warning: the landscape can be bewildering, so a local guide is virtually essential.

Access to Coyote Buttes, which lies within the Paria Canyon-Vermilion Cliffs Wilderness area to the west of the Paria River, is strictly controlled, partly via a permit lottery system, to help protect the fragile formations. While waiting for your number to come up, a fantastic adventure can be had near Page in Cardiac Canyon and Canyon X. Two of Arizona's numerous slot canyons (sheer-walled and very narrow sandstone chasms that can be hundreds of feet high), they can make an

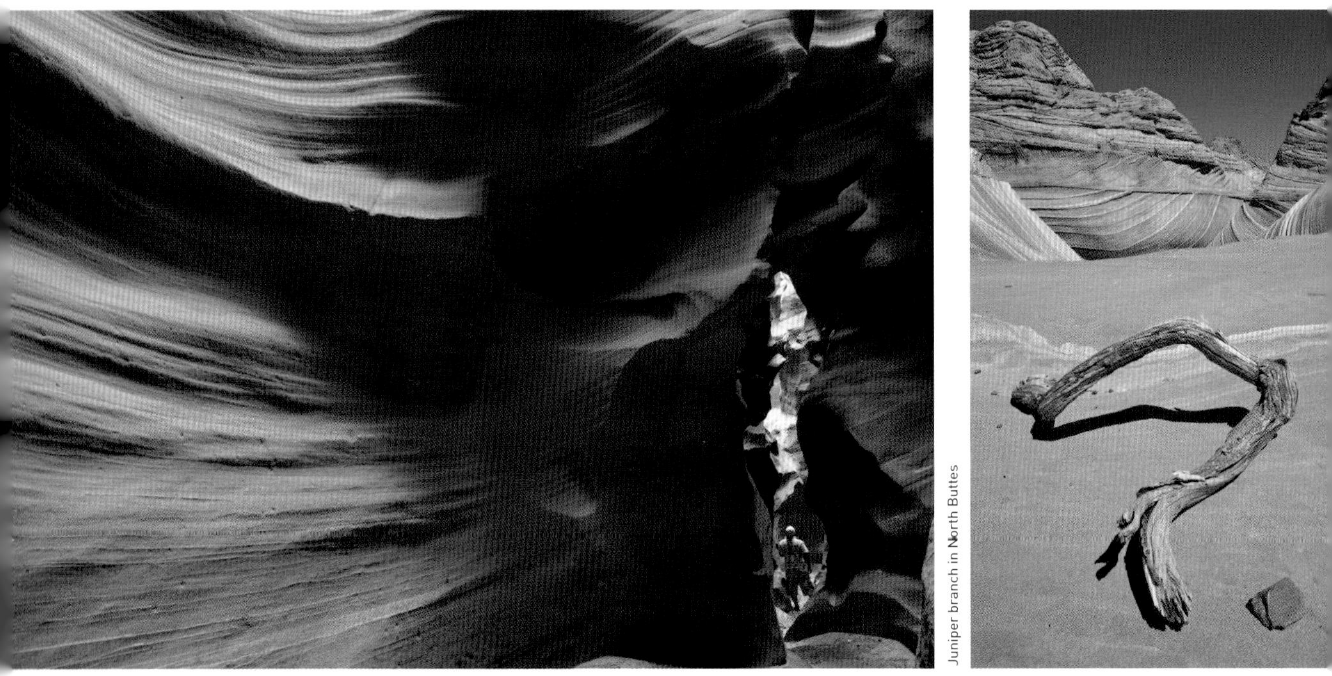
Juniper branch in North Buttes

Slots and rock waves in Cardiac Canyon

excellent one-day hike. The adjoining Antelope Canyon is the most famous slot canyon, but it is often overrun with tour groups who are marched through on a feature-list-ticking time schedule. In contrast, Cardiac and X are so far off the beaten track, on Navajo reservation land, that they are almost a secret, even though they are every bit as mesmerizing as their more illustrious neighbour.

It is often hard to see slot canyons from ground level until you stumble right upon them. And when you stare into the deep chasm of

Cardiac Canyon, dark as a moonless night at the bottom, it seems like a gateway to the centre of the Earth. It is impossible to penetrate many slots without ropes, but here the route in is a fun-filled scree run down a steep gully. The searing desert temperatures of the surface drop noticeably as you descend into the shade of the canyon walls.

Craning your neck to glimpse the top of the cliffs soon becomes futile in the ever shrinking entrance to the slot itself. Barely wider

Colourful rocks in South Buttes

Life on the rocks, North Buttes

The Teepees at South Buttes

than a hotel corridor to start with, the trail is swallowed by the overbearing rose-coloured sandstone walls of the gorge, then narrows down to shoulder width or less. The sculpted rock melts and merges into waves, lips, scoops and twirls, like those made by a warm spoon run repeatedly through a tub of ice cream.

A short hike through a wider part, or wash, of the canyon system links into Canyon X. Rarely seen by outsiders, or even by the Navajo

Gnarled juniper branch at South Buttes

Morning light at South Buttes

themselves, for whom the great owls that reside in it are bad omens, it is very different to Cardiac. Halfway through, the slot becomes a tunnel with only dapples of light creeping through tiny rock windows above. The intensity of the colours rippling across the wavy sandstone reaches new depths before you emerge for the scramble back up to the blinding brightness and sapping heat of the surface world.

The Coyote Buttes area is split in two: the South Buttes and the North Buttes. The most popular attraction is the Wave, in the northern half. A 4.8-km hike from the Wire Pass trail head – off Highway 89 to

Crazy 'brain' paving at White Pockets

Kanab – across a trail-less area of dunes and rock outcrops, it is a riot of cross-bedded, multicoloured sandstone. The main formation is the bowl, where the perfectly smoothed rock sweeps up high on all sides like a petrified sea in a violent storm. Visitor numbers are severely restricted here – just 20 people a day are allowed into the North Buttes – but the small size of the Wave area, and the fragility of its surface, leave no doubt that such controls are essential.

A short drive east, before you arrive at the South Buttes, takes you to the unheralded White Pockets area, perhaps the most astonishing of all the rock formations. A thin sheet of white sandstone, formed into brain-like blocks and mounds, overlays the region's more predominant red sandstone and some layers of banana-yellow rock. Where the three mix, they create a visual feast of white, pink, cream and cappuccino-brown swirls that really do look good enough to eat.

The South Buttes are more difficult to access than the North Buttes (a 4WD vehicle is necessary), but it is generally easier to secure permits for them. One of their most beautiful features is the Teepees, an

Dusk light at White Pockets

Sunrise at White Pockets

Coffee-coloured rock swirls dominate at White Pockets

isolated huddle of conical hills that glow golden in the early morning and late afternoon sun. Exploring further, behind the Teepees, reveals precariously balanced sandstone spires, delicate rock fins and ancient, gnarled juniper trees. With extensive views over the entire Paria Canyon-Vermilion Cliffs Wilderness area and Bryce Canyon far to the north, this is a perfect place to sit and contemplate an extraordinary landscape that has been 200 million years in the making.

ⓘ

Hiking takes place year-round, but the summer months can be searingly hot. Flash floods are most likely in July, August and September. Overland Canyon Tours, based in Page, is the only company with Navajo permission to enter Cardiac Canyon and Canyon X. It arranges tailor-made trips to all the main formations. Half the permits for Coyote Buttes are available at the Arizona Bureau of Land Management website, but are snapped up quickly. The remainder are allocated at the daily permit lottery at the Paria Ranger Station. Lotteries for the Wave are heavily oversubscribed, so plan well ahead. Arizona Tourism can advise on travel arrangements, and the Page Boy Hotel is an affordable base.

6
4
24
21
11
15
12
14
10
27
2
20
8
26
5
23
19
13
17
25
16
28
3

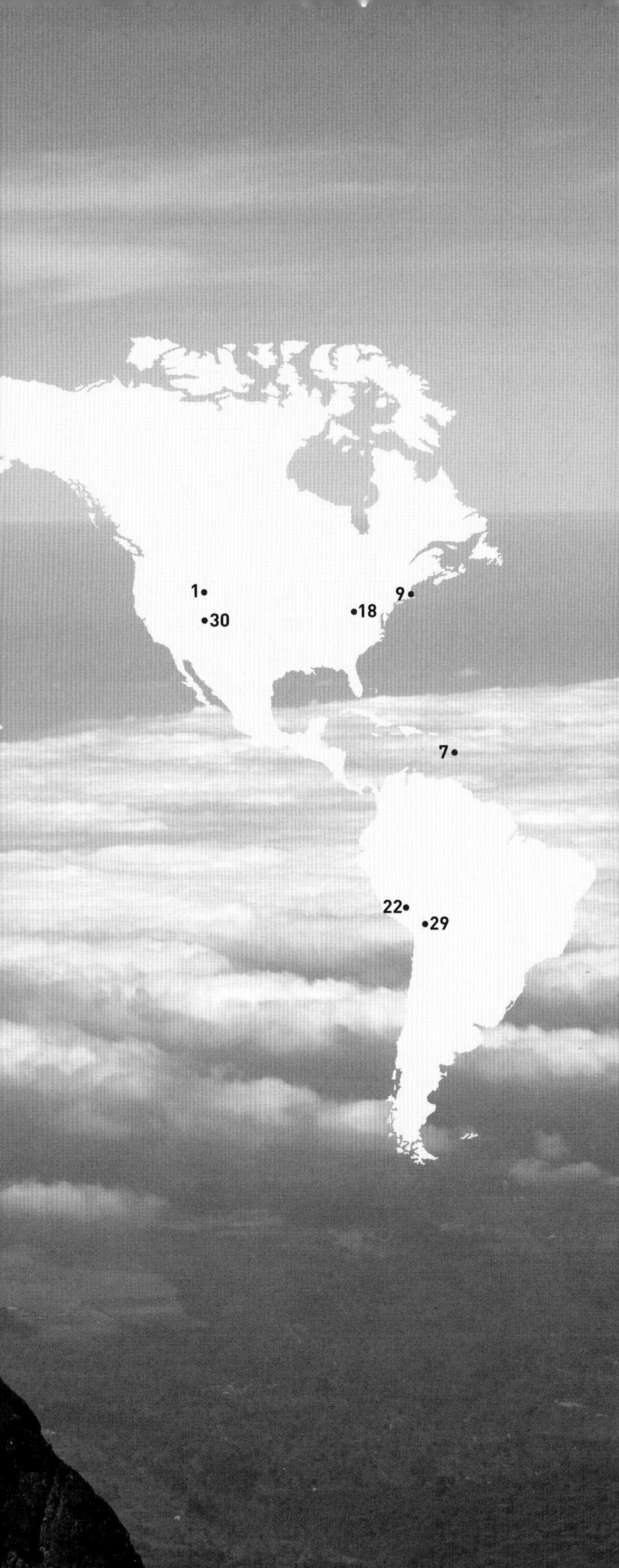

1
30
18
9
7
22
29

1 YELLOWSTONE NATIONAL PARK, USA
2 AMALFI COAST, ITALY
3 THE ROUTEBURN TRACK, NEW ZEALAND
4 WEST HIGHLAND WAY, SCOTLAND
5 TEMPLES OF KYOTO, JAPAN
6 LOFOTEN ISLANDS, NORWAY
7 MORNE TROIS PITONS, DOMINICA
8 DROVERS' ROADS, SPAIN
9 BOSTON'S FREEDOM TRAIL, USA
10 TOUR DU MONT BLANC, EUROPE
11 SOUTH WEST COAST PATH, ENGLAND
12 KING LUDWIG'S WAY, GERMANY
13 TIGER LEAPING GORGE, CHINA
14 THE DOLOMITES, ITALY
15 BATTLEFIELDS OF THE SOMME, FRANCE
16 GARDEN ROUTE, SOUTH AFRICA
17 DOGON COUNTRY, MALI
18 FALLINGWATER, USA
19 DARJEELING TEA TREK, INDIA
20 METEORA, GREECE
21 CANALS OF AMSTERDAM, NETHERLANDS
22 INCA TRAIL, PERU
23 WOLONG NATURE RESERVE, CHINA
24 COAST TO COAST, ENGLAND
25 MOUNT KILIMANJARO, TANZANIA
26 THE LYCIAN WAY, TURKEY
27 KARST COUNTRY, SLOVENIA
28 GREAT OCEAN WALK, AUSTRALIA
29 TAKESI TRAIL, BOLIVIA
30 COYOTE BUTTES, USA

Useful web addresses

Yellowstone National Park, USA

National Park Service – US Department of the Interior
www.nps.gov/yell/
Tel: +1 307 344 7381

Amalfi Coast, Italy

Landscapes of Sorrento, Amalfi and Capri – Car Tours and Walks by Julian Tippett
www.sunflowerbooks.co.uk

Italian State Tourist Board
www.enit.it

The Routeburn Track, New Zealand

New Zealand Tourist Board
www.newzealand.com

Air New Zealand
www.airnewzealand.com

Ultimate Hikes
www.ultimatehikes.co.nz
Tel: +64 3 442 8200

West Highland Way, Scotland

Macs Adventure
www.macsadventure.com
Tel: +44 (0) 141 248 2323

Visit Scotland
www.visitscotland.com

Temples of Kyoto, Japan

ANA
www.anaskyweb.com
Tel: +44 (0) 870 837 8866

Japan National Tourist Organization
www.jnto.go.jp
www.seejapan.co.uk

Lofoten Islands, Norway

Inntravel
www.inntravel.com
Tel: +44 (0) 1653 617949

SAS – Scandinavian Airlines
www.flysas.com
Tel: 0871 521 2772 (UK only)

Norwegian Tourist Board
www.visitnorway.com

Morne Trois Pitons, Dominica

Dominica Tourism
www.dominica.dm
Tel: 0800 012 1467
(Toll free – UK only)
Tel: 1 866 522 4057
(Toll free – USA & Canada only)

British Airways
www.ba.com
Tel: 0870 850 9850 (UK only)

Evergreen Hotel
www.avirtualdominica.com/evergreen
Tel: +1 767 448 3288

Papillote Wilderness Retreat
www.papillote.dm
Tel: +1 767 448 2287

Rainforest Shangri-la Resort
www.rainforestshangrilaresort.com
Tel: +1 767 440 5093

Titiwi Inn
www.titiwi.com
Tel: +1 767 448 0553

Drovers' Roads, Andalucia, Spain

Andalucian Adventures
www.andalucian-adventures.co.uk
Tel: +44 (0) 1453 834137

Andalucia Tourist Board
www.andalucia.org

Boston's Freedom Trail, USA

The Freedom Trail Foundation
www.thefreedomtrail.org
Tel: +1 617 357 8300

Greater Boston Convention & Visitors Bureau
www.bostonusa.com

Tour du Mont Blanc, Europe

Sherpa Expeditions
www.sherpa-walking-holidays.co.uk
Tel: +44 (0) 20 8577 2717

French Tourist Office
www.francetourism.com

Italian State Tourist Board
www.enit.it

Swiss Tourist Office
www.myswitzerland.com

South West Coast Path, England

South West Coast Path Team
www.southwestcoastpath.com
Tel: +44 (0) 1392 383560

England Tourist Board
www.enjoyengland.com

King Ludwig's Way, Germany

Sherpa Expeditions
www.sherpa-walking-holidays.co.uk
Tel: +44 (0) 20 8577 2717

German Tourist Board
www.germany-tourism.de

Tiger Leaping Gorge, China

In Depth China
www.indepthchina.com
Tel: +86 888 3101228

China National Tourist Office
www.cnto.org

The Dolomites, Italy

Collett's Mountain Holidays
www.colletts.co.uk
Tel: +44 (0) 1763 289660

Italian Tourist Board
www.enit.it

Battlefields of the Somme, France

Commonwealth War Graves Commission
www.cwgc.org

Walking the Somme by Paul Reed
www.somme-1916.com

Bernafay Wood B&B
http://cf.geocities.com/bed_and_breakfast_bernafay_wood/index
Tel: +33 (0) 3 22 85 02 47

French Tourist Office
www.francetourism.com

Garden Route, South Africa

South Africa Tourist Board
www.southafrica.net

Oystercatcher Trail
www.oystercatchertrail.co.za
Tel: +27 (0) 44 699 1204

Garden Route Trail
www.gardenroutetrail.co.za
Tel: +27 (0) 44 883 1015

Gamkaberg Nature Reserve
www.capenature.co.za

Knysna Tourism
www.tourismknysna.co.za

African Breeze Guest House (Knysna)
www.africanbreezeguesthouse.co.za
Tel: +27 (0) 44 384 0157

George Tourism
www.tourismgeorge.co.za

Wilderness Tourist Bureau
www.tourismwilderness.co.za

Malvern Manor
www.malvernmanor.co.za

Dogon Country, Mali

Tim Best Travel
www.timbesttravel.com
Tel: +44 (0) 20 7591 0300
US Toll Free: 1866 5123091

Fallingwater, USA

Fallingwater – Western Pennsylvania Conservancy
www.paconserve.org/index-fw1.asp
Tel: +1 724 329 8501

Pennsylvania Tourism
www.visitpa.com

Stepping Stone Farm B&B, Confluence
Tel: +1 814 395 9988
www.steppingstonefarmbnb.com

Darjeeling Tea Trek, India

Tim Best Travel
www.timbesttravel.com
Tel: +44 (0) 20 7591 0300
US Toll Free: 1866 5123091

Incredible India (Ministry of Tourism)
www.incredibleindia.org

Glenburn Tea Estate
www.glenburnteaestate.com

Meteora, Greece

Greek National Tourism Organization
www.visitgreece.gr

Konstantina Papaefthimiou (licensed English-speaking guide)
Email: konstantipap@yahoo.gr
Tel: +30 2410 235297

Canals of Amsterdam, The Netherlands

Netherlands Board of Tourism & Conventions
www.holland.com

Amsterdam Tourism & Convention Board
www.amsterdamtourist.nl
Tel: +31 (0) 20 551 2525

Mövenpick Hotel
www.moevenpick-hotels.com/hotels/Amsterdam/welcome.htm
Tel: +31 (0) 20 519 1200

Inca Trail, Peru

Abercrombie & Kent
www.abercrombiekent.co.uk
Tel: 0845 618 2200 (UK callers only)
Tel: +44 01242 547700 (overseas callers)

Peru Tourism Board
www.peru.info

Wolong Nature Reserve, China

Panda Travel & Tour Consultant
www.chinagiantpanda.com

China National Tourist Office
www.cnto.org

Coast to Coast, England

England Tourist Board
www.enjoyengland.com

Coast 2 Coast
www.coast2coast.co.uk
Tel: +44 (0) 1609 883 731

Mount Kilimanjaro, Tanzania

High & Wild
www.highandwild.co.uk
Tel: +44 (0) 1749 671777

Tanzania Tourist Board
www.tanzaniatouristboard.com

The Lycian Way, Turkey

On Foot Holidays
www.onfootholidays.co.uk
Tel: +44 (0) 1722 322652

Turkey Tourism Board
www.tourismturkey.org

Karst Country, Slovenia

On Foot Holidays
www.onfootholidays.co.uk
Tel: +44 (0) 1722 322652

Slovenia Tourist Board
www.slovenia.info

Great Ocean Walk, Australia

Auswalk
www.auswalk.com.au
Tel: +61 03 5356 4971

Australia Travel & Tourism
www.australia.com

Takesi Trail, Bolivia

Tim Best Travel
www.timbesttravel.com
Tel: +44 (0) 20 7591 0300
US Toll Free: 1866 5123091

Coyote Buttes, USA

Arizona Office of Tourism
www.arizonaguide.com
Tel: +1 866 275 5816

Page-Lake Powell Tourism Bureau
www.pagelakepowelltourism.com

Overland Canyon Tours
www.overlandcanyontours.com
Tel: +1 928 608 4072

Page Boy Motel
www.pageboymotel.us
Tel: +1 928 645 2416

A FIREFLY BOOK

Published by Firefly Books Ltd. 2008

First printing

Publisher Cataloging-in-Publication Data (U.S.)

Watkins, Steve.
Unforgettable walks to take before you die / Steve Watkins; and Clare Jones.
[256] p. : col. photos., maps ; cm.
Summary: Long and short, leisurely and demanding walks throughout the world. These include: Boston's Freedom Trail and the temples of Kyoto, the open countryside of the Yellowstone National Park, Peru's Inca Trail, Frank Lloyd Wright's Fallingwater property, a stroll around the canals of Amsterdam, the Alpine Tour du Mont Blanc and China's Tiger Leaping Gorge trek.
ISBN-13: 978-1-55407-428-0 (pbk.)
ISBN-10: 1-55407-428-2 (pbk.)
1. Walking — Guidebooks. 2. Hiking — Guidebooks. I. Jones, Clare. II. Title.
796.51 dc22 GV199.5.W385 2008

Library and Archives Canada Cataloguing in Publication

Watkins, Steve
Unforgettable walks to take before you die / Steve Watkins and Clare Jones.
ISBN-13: 978-1-55407-428-0
ISBN-10: 1-55407-428-2
1. Walking — Guidebooks. 2. Hiking — Guidebooks. I. Jones, Clare II. Title.
GV199.5.W37 2008 796.51 C2008-901101-5

Published in the United States by
Firefly Books (U.S.) Inc.
P.O. Box 1338, Ellicott Station
Buffalo, New York 14205

Published in Canada by
Firefly Books Ltd.
66 Leek Crescent
Richmond Hill, Ontario L4B 1H1

For The Random House Group Limited
Commissioning editor: Christopher Tinker
Copyeditor: Tessa Clark
Designer: Bobby Birchall, Bobby&Co, London
Production controller: Antony Heller

Set in DIN Regular
Cover images © Steve Watkins and Clare Jones.
Front: "The Wave", Coyote Buttes, Arizona, United States; Back: "Evening at Grand Prismatic Spring", Yellowstone National Park, Wyoming, United States; Front Flap: "Giant Bamboo Forest", Temples of Kyoto, Kyoto, Japan

Printed in China

For Lewis Michael Watkins, who couldn't be with us but still brought sunshine and rainbows every step of the way.

Acknowledgements

Steve and Clare would in particular like to thank Christopher Tinker, Nicky Ross and Antony Heller at BBC Books, Bobby Birchall at Bobby&Co, Tessa Clark and Helen Armitage for their invaluable work and support in bringing this book together.

They would also like to thank the following people for their support, advice and assistance with organizing trips and for sharing their laughter and friendship over the many kilometres walked: John Brough, David Lanfear, Rhys Henderson at Salomon, Linda Lashford, Jo Carter, Roger Jones, Neil Lapping, Bianca Barker, Kenny Sutherland, David Holmes, Katia Vignes, Sian Pritchard-Jones, Bob Gibbons, Rianne Steenbergen, Sophie Palmer, Hana Keegan, Ela Keegan, Jane Keegan, Roy Keegan, Joke Herngreen, Maarten Coolen, Manos Hatzimalonas, Konstantina Papaefthimiou, George Vlachoyiannis, Helias Vlachoyiannis, Lindsey McNally, Philip Nelson, Elaine and Owen Jones, Katrina Milne Holme, Claire Hilton, Fernando Piaggio, Tim Best, Oliver Alvestegui, Bree Simms, Laura Legetter, Fred Orban, Jenny Nothard, Willie Komani, Cornelius Julies, Tom Barry, Mark Dixon, Simon and Cathy Warren, Craig Nancarrow, Aneli Esterhuizen, Sandra and Michael Cook, Joan Shaw, Eben Lourens, Mr M.V. Babu, Miranda Boord, Peter Yourgyal, Dawa Sherpa, Issie Ingles, Sanjay R. Sharma, Heather Mollins, Louise Cummins, Alison Greenhalgh, Steve Greenhalgh, Ollie Greenhalgh, Josh Riddell, Ashley 'Wha' Murphy, Miri Bartlett, Nick Cunliffe, Surf-Lines, Sheila Nelson, Frank Nelson, Bryn Jones, Fflur Roberts, Sarah Gooding, Mel Watkins, Dilys Watkins, Kylie Clark, Mayu Okamoto, Julia Spence, Rebecca Bruce, Matilda Granville; Susan and Andrew Collingbourne; Charly Moore, David Rankin, Dwayne Cassidy, Pearl Macek, Susie Tempest, Margel Durand, Marvlyn Alexander-James, Keith and Janet Heath; Fred Phillips and Dr Janet Taylor; Jerry Fu and John; Matt, Lisa, Jon and Tom at Collett's; Mary Pocock, Simon Scutt, Monica Coleman; Alan Dow and Yvonne; Clinton Piper; Nigel Gifford, Caroline Grayburn, Baye; Graham, Farah, Aliyah and Suraya Bond; Pete, Kirsty, Oscar and Angus Dart; Guy, Ani, Will and Sam Alma; Keith Byrne at the North Face.